The Pursuit of Passion
How to Sequence your Life for Success

Tiffany Jerome

An imprint of Kenneth Wyche Publishing

Kenneth Wyche Publishing ©

Part of and in association with lifewithken.com

First published in the United States by Kenneth Wyche Publishing.

Any names, characters, or places depicted are strictly allegorical in nature with no real-world implications and are most cases fictional.

Copyright © Kenneth Wyche Publishing

All rights reserved no part of this book may be reproduced or used in any manner without written permission from the copyright owner except for the use of quotations in a book review.

The moral rights of the author have been asserted
The publisher does not have any control over and does not assume responsibility for the author or third-party websites or their content.

978-1-7374408-2-6 (Paperback)
978-1-7374408-0-2 (eBook)
978-1-7374408-1-9 (Hardcover)

To those going through the process of commitment and healing. What you are committed to you will find success in. And what you are being healed of can no longer ale you.

Table of Contents

Introduction i

Chapter 1 Health is Wealth 1

Chapter 2 Finances 14

Chapter 3 Fitness 38

Chapter 4 Future 59

Chapter 5 Living in Alignment 70

Chapter 6 The Power of a Breakthrough 96

Chapter 7 Who are You? 103

Chapter 8 The Man Who Chose to Live Out of Alignment 123

Chapter 9 Mental Health Matters 131

Chapter 10 Relationships 140

Chapter 11 The Business of Life 159

Chapter 12 Heavy is the Head 167

Conclusion 172

Acknowledgments

About the Author

Introduction

Have you ever gone out of your way for someone, putting in a decent amount of your time and effort just for your deed to go unnoticed or underappreciated? Maybe you find yourself in a position where you hate Sundays because all that means is tomorrow's Monday. Or is it you feel as though you are not where you think you should be in life right now? All of these things are byproducts of living out of alignment.

"Living in Alignment" means that the entirety of your being is in sync with itself. It means that there is uniformity in your existence. The examples I gave are symptoms of not living in this way. Your mind, body, spirit, and resources are the gateways through which you experience the world around you. If one of those things are not in alignment it will manifest itself in ways that may seem frustrating, inconvenient, unfair, upsetting, or downright wrong.

Even though we wrestle with the unpredictability of life, how you conduct yourself in your existence will determine how bumpy the road will be for you. It's likely you may know someone who keeps making the same mistakes over and over again, and subsequently, keeps getting hurt by their own decisions. Have you ever been in over your head in a situation? I know I have. Sometimes you can put yourself in bad situations because you do not take yourself into consideration.

How many times have you taken a job just because "you needed the money"? How many times have you done something that you knew you should not have done? These are things that people do to themselves all the time. The problem with living like this is that this road leads to nowhere, fast. Before you know it, you will find yourself in a predetermined routine that will become more difficult for you to break away from as you become more accustomed to it. Now there is nothing wrong if that routine is a reflection of who you are; Routines are an important part of

Living in Alignment. The value in a routine, however, is whether or not that routine is life giving.

How is your routine serving you in a proactive way? Is every day a new opportunity, or are you watching the clock, waiting for the day to end as soon as your alarm goes off in the morning? A good routine should be one that is refreshing and not draining. That is what Living in Alignment is intrinsically about: living a life that reflects your true identity. The world has been designed to rob people of their individuality. As early as kindergarten you are taught to behave in a certain way; and those that do not are considered "problematic." We have been indoctrinated with societal norms that historically have not had our best interests in mind.

I will be honest; I am still waiting for that moment when I will not always have a calculator on me. While schools are busy teaching math, science, and reading, they tend to skip over teaching things that help students understand, experience, and explore self-expression. I believe that if students had an opportunity to find themselves throughout middle school and high school, they would not waste money trying to do so in college. The journey to discovering and understanding yourself can be arduous, so it would be in your best interest to work with yourself and not against yourself.

That is what this book is designed to teach you to do. Before I started living in a way that truly represented my thoughts, desires, dreams, and passions, I spent most of my time living for other people. By the time I would clocked out of work, I only had two definitive things to look forward to: the drive home, and sometimes dinner (depending on what I felt like eating on any given night). I used to never give myself any time out of my own day. I committed myself to the needs of others, and thought that somehow, by giving myself over to helping other people, I would receive the help I needed in return. This line of thinking was erroneous to say the least. By living for my job, friends, and family, I did not give myself any time to live for myself. Additionally, by doing things for the purpose of pleasing others, I never allowed myself the time to address the things lacking in my life that would ultimately bring me pleasure.

In addition to depriving myself of the value of a life that is centered around my own happiness, I also found myself on the receiving end of several rude awakenings when one after another, people would inevitably let me down. After enough hurt, pain, remorse, and resentment, I realized that you cannot give people anything that they do not want. What I mean by this is, the same reason why you are reading this book, is the same reason why someone else is not. You cannot force people to make a change, you cannot force people to accept you, and you cannot force people to value your input. The people around you may not like what you have to say, but that does not mean you should not say it anyway.

After having that revelation, I accepted that the only way for people to find value in me is for me to find value in me. That is when I started focusing my energies on manifesting my desires. I raised my own stock price. I decided that I am worthy enough to respect myself, and it's from that place of self-respect how I chose and choose to live my life every day. I took all the various aspects of myself and asked myself a simple question: Which of these parts are not like the other? I inspected and took inventory of my life. Not necessarily knowing what I was looking for, but willing to confront whatever it was I may have found.

The concept of Living in Alignment was birthed in me when I discovered a way to live that represents (is in alignment with) my spirit, mind, body, and resources. The secret to this discovery is in understanding your needs in relation to your goals. Without vision you will perish. To live in alignment you must be aligned, or in right position. This starts with the desires of your heart. What is it that you truly want? Uncovering that mystery can be a feat in and of itself however, your desires would not have been put in you if they were not meant to be fulfilled through you.

You are a spiritual being having a physical experience meaning, you interact with the world not only physically, materially, and emotionally, but supernaturally as well. Living in Alignment means that you have one agenda that informs these key aspects of your existence. The best way you can begin to acknowledge and develop this agenda is by grappling with what you want out of the totality of your life. For a lot of us, this fight starts with our spirit man. There is nothing wrong with wanting something, the value however is in the reason why you want that something. If your reasoning is not matching up with your results, that is a tell-tell sign, that you are not doing what is in your best interest.

    The sad reality is a lot of people live like this every day-stuck doing whatever it is they are doing. When you do this, you keep yourself from getting to your compelling future: the reality that would make you most happy. It's my goal to show you how to systematically get out of this rut. By following what I have outlined in this book, you can begin to be the change you want to see, not only in your life, but in the world around you.

People want to have something to believe in, and they will gravitate towards individuality. As much as we are all the "same," those that express their uniqueness are the ones who get spotlighted. Maybe you are meant to be in the spotlight among your family, coworkers, a significant other, friend group, and/or social environment. Maybe you are the hope that other people need to be who they want to be as well. It's time to realize your potential. The era in your life of selling yourself short is over. Now is the time for you to be the amazing individual that you are. Now is the time for you to pursue your passion!

Chapter 1

Health is Wealth

There are only two directions a person can go in life: forward, and nowhere. The natural progression of life is forward moving. For something to be alive it must be growing. This sentiment is not only true externally, but internally as well. You can gauge the health of various areas of your life by whether or not you can identify growth or a lack thereof.

All of us have different aspects of ourselves that are a reflection of who we are. The best illustration for this is your own individual buying power. Where and how you spend your money represents what you value. There are people who only buy a certain type of coffee for example, because they value that coffee drinking experience. There are people who only buy a specific brand of car because they value driving that particular manufacturer. Brand value matters. People tend to think however, that a brand is an outside force from the perspective of influence.

People live in such a way that they allow life to happen to them. They are reactionary, only capable of responding and not acting upon. A brand is not only something that you respond to, but also something that you can act upon. You do not only have the choice of whether or not you like a certain product, but you also have the choice of what you are going to do about it. As this relates to yourself, you can choose to be more than a victim of your circumstance.

Growing up all people ever did was tell me who I was, what I was good for, and what I was capable of. But no one had the courage or insight to ask me what I was going to do about it. The number one power that you have is the ability to dictate the course of your life. Just because you grew up wearing one brand of shoes your whole life does not mean that tomorrow you cannot go out and buy a different one. Just because you may come from somewhere that did not set you up to succeed in life, does not mean that you cannot make your dreams a reality. And just because someone has an opinion about your life, does not mean that they have the facts of your life. You wield the branding power of your life.

It's your own personal brand that impacts the material aspects of your life that matter. From how you socialize, to how you spend your money, to how you treat yourself when no one is around. Who you are is reflected in all that you do. Every day we materialize the world around us—we manifest what we experience. Your life is the projector of your subconscious.

Imagine being at a birthday party and everyone is having a good time. All of a sudden, a party guest just starts flipping out. This guest got upset over an issue not related to the birthday. So, while everyone is trying to have a good time, there is this one person who cannot seem to get his act together, and he is distracting everyone from enjoying themselves. Because we do not know the details of the situation we cannot remark on the justification or lack thereof for this party disrupter's behavior; however, it's obvious that this person chose to behave this way for a reason. And it's his behavior that elicits a poor response from his environment.

You set the tone of your life. You decide whether or not you fade into obscurity or propel yourself into freedom. Life will conform to your will if you are willing to bend it. This is a core principle of Living in Alignment, living in such a way that life happens for you and not to you.

You become the brand ambassador of your life by making choices that have a material impact. Who you are is predicated on your rate of growth. How healthy is your life? You know something is healthy by whether or not it's growing. You know your life is growing based on what materializes around you. And what materializes in your life generally comes in the form of relationships, personal development, material things or "stuff," and subjective success. You can know how well you are doing in life simply by taking stock of what you currently have.

What is key to note here is that the area in which you can identify the most growth, is not as important as growth taking place in general. A fact of life is that somethings grow faster than others, and a subjective truth is not everyone values the same thing at every stage of their life. As a 30-year-old, growing a career may be more important than having robust relationships. As a 20-year-old, having a bunch of friends is probably more important than retiring comfortably. The illusiveness of success is that it's subjective—what makes one person seem or feel successful may be different for someone else.

That is why success is a pursuit of passion rooted in one's "material health." Your material health is an amalgamation of "things" that contribute to the tangible state of your existence. It's comprised of the three F's: your Fitness,

Finances, and Future. Fitness does not solely refer to physical health, but rather the general wellbeing of your overall health—of which, does include your physical health. Your finances are the vehicle by which you get to where you want to be in life; and your future is what you plan on doing once you get there.

These three aspects of yourself are essential to fully realizing the pinnacle of your potential (success). Living in Alignment will cause you to incrementally build on the progression of your life via your material health, so that you can act on your personal brand and create the life you want for yourself.

There once was a man who found himself working at a dead-end job. This man was 34 years old and previously unemployed. He graduated with a master's degree and was hoping that the prolonged time he spent in school would make room for him to be able to find a high paying job. This man struggled for two years after graduating to find something that he found interesting and that was in his field. When he finally found an opportunity, though it was not under the purview of his degree, he was remotely interested in the job, and he would have been making more than the nothing he was making before. The role was great at first, the work itself was not all that exhilarating but Roy was the type of guy to keep his head down and lie below the radar. Roy hoped that he would be able to grow in this role and then carry the learned experience elsewhere.

Once the honeymoon phase wore off Roy began to realize that the job was not all peaches and roses. His life was slowly beginning to fall apart. Things that used to not bother him started bothering him. He had less time for himself because he was always working overtime and never because he wanted to. Eventually he realized that he was not happy, but he had gotten so used to his lifestyle that he could not fathom living any other way (plus the fear of unemployment lingered in the back of his mind). Roy tried asking for a promotion once, and he was offered one when one would become available. One has yet to become available and Roy has yet to find the will to do something else with his life.

Stephanie was 40 years old and engaged. She was a career woman and wanted to wait until she reached the apex of her career to start a family. Once she had done so she decided she was ready to get married to her longtime boyfriend Craig. They even decided to freeze some of Stephanie's eggs to ensure that they could still have a family. Jessica, Stephanie's friend since high school and lifelong partner in crime could not even be in the same room with a child. Jessica was a "doing things my own way" kind of person. The two were all each other had outside of their nuclear families. As Stephanie continued to excel in her life, Jessica for the most part did not make any significant leaps or bounds. Eventually it came to the point where neither had much really to talk about with each other anymore. They still valued each other's company, but their lives had become too different and neither put in the effort to grow and mature their friendship.

We all run the risk of finding ourselves in a position in life where an aspect of ourselves is not growing. When someone is not growing in an area of their life that matters to them, they lose resolve. Why would someone want more for themselves when they cannot see more for themselves? When growth stops vision stops, and when vision stops the person perishes. When you do not have something to focus on you do not have something to hope for. Roy lost his resolve because he allowed life to rule him. He could not see past his past. Stephanie and Jessica's friendship stopped growing because the two decided to stop working on it. "What was" will not always be "what is," and "what is" eventually has to become "what is next(?)." Without growth and progress, we all run the risk of perishing right where we are.

In an alternative universe Roy would have come to his senses and found a way to leave that job so that he could do something more self-gratifying. In that same alternate universe Jessica and Stephanie would have spent more time together, picked up new hobbies, and found ways to better support one another. The right thing to do is always the easiest to conclude to yet the most difficult to act on. This is why people fail. They are not successful at being consistent. Consistency is the secret ingredient to the success pie. The key to consistency is not whether or not a person is consistent, it's what that person is consistent in doing.

Success leaves trails, and regardless of what you want your life to look like by the time you finish reading this book the truth is, you are going to have to follow a success trail. This means, that there will be no excuse for where you are in life aside from a lack of consistent effort. This is why so few people are successful. What are you doing on a regular basis that is getting you closer to your goals? That is the formula to growth. There is no get rich quick scheme for success. Success is maintained not attained. Throughout this book I am going to show you how to maintain a certain level of success in your life.

The actions that you take to be successful may look different for you compared to someone else, but there are core principles that you must ascertain if you ever want to achieve your compelling future. Your compelling future is your vision from within. It's your desires. The word desire means "of the Father." "Father" in this sense equates to God or the universe. What you desire, what you are passionate about, and what you find pleasure in is meant to be in your life. It would not have been put on your heart if it was not meant to come to fruition in your life. The best way to get vision is by starting with whatever it is you already want. Your goal is to follow the clues left in your life.

The reason why you want to have a compelling future is because this is where your legacy is. Your legacy is how you are remembered. I would highly recommend that if you do not already, that you place high value on the mark that you are going to leave on this world. The idea of who you are predicates a future. To be someone you must already be being someone. It does not matter whether or not you intend on leaving a legacy, the fact that you are alive affirms that your legacy is already being left. It's not whether or not you will be in the history books; it's about who you will be in those books.

In its simplest form, a legacy makes life worth it. It gives people something to live for. Aside from providing a vision, legacy also gives your life longevity. Once again however, outliving yourself should be a self-identified desire. From a humanistic and evolutionary perspective, outliving ourselves through the creation of more of ourselves in the form of children is fundamental. If one of the purposes of life is to produce, wouldn't it be nice to produce something that has intrinsic value? Something that is more than the sum of its parts yet is in part an extension of you? That does not have to look like having kids—to each is own; remember success is subjective. But within the context of your material health, it's possible to create a lasting impact that can have a ripple affect across a generation.

This is why your fitness, finances, and future, are so important, because it's through these mediums that we affect the world. Sequencing your life for success is about being intentional in growing in these areas of your life. These areas of your life are identified as important because these are the parts of you that you manifest. You can enact your will on what does and does not grow in your life. You decide the purpose money has in your life and the way you respond to that belief. You choose whether or not your future is worth it. By making decisions about these areas of your life that reflect who you are, you place yourself in the driver seat. Yes, life is unpredictable, that is a characteristic of it however, you do not have to live in instability or inferiority. You can be all that you are meant to be regardless of what may come up against you. Once you become skilled in making life happen for you the only obstacle standing in your way will be yourself. Anyone can be successful, but not everyone is willing. Are you?

Chapter 2

<u>Finances</u>

The first "F" that I want to cover is your finances. Your finances are an essential part of your material health. For the most part, a majority of people live in a society that requires buying and selling. Transactions are how we do business and operate with the world around us. The most obvious way in which we conduct transactions is through our buying power.

The first thing that I want you to get, is that you have to get comfortable with talking about money. The intentionality behind starting with this subject is so that we can break the ice. I do not know you personally, but we can all relate to money. In western civilization (specifically not exclusively) money has been deified. People turn to it for strength, a sense of self, comfort, and confidence. People think that money will solve all their problems, and that if they had more of it, they would be happier. The truth of the matter is your money is only as good as how you use it. A person can have a distorted relationship with money when they do not see it as an extension of themselves.

A good example of this is the stereotypical story of the person who wins the lottery for millions of dollars and by the time the year is over they are worse off than before they had the money. This is because that person thought money would change their life when in reality, all money did was enter their life. Society sells us this false narrative about wealth and success. What you have is only as good as what you do with it. That is why one man's trash can be another man's treasure. The same is the case with money. I hate to break it to you, but money in and of itself is not real.

If you take a $100 bill and examine it, you will notice that it's made of paper. While paper is a derivative of a living organism it in and of itself is not a living organism. Humans give money life. Money does not have an intrinsic heartbeat; people give it one—and check on its condition every day via the stock market. Your relationship with money is important because it will determine how much you inevitably have; and how much you have will inevitably depend on the value you place on it. Your attitude can either attract or repel money to your life. It's not enough to have/want money; you have to learn to respect it as well.

Everything is matter, and matter is made up of molecules. Molecules are made up of atoms which are made up of protons and neutrons. The point that I want to get at is that on a molecular level, everything is in constant motion. And since molecules make up the world, everything around us is therefore in constant motion as well. Molecules expand and condense materializing in every variation of anything that is solid, gaseous, or liquid. From a molecular perspective, humans are in constant motion also. The cells in our bodies are made up of millions of molecules.

This is key to understanding the universal Law of Vibration. This law states that everything is energy, and that everything moves and vibrates. The intrinsic value in this law is that everything vibrates, but, at its own frequency. This is relevant because it means that you get to interact with things in part because they have a different frequency (structural composition) than you. Because you are a sentient being, you have the power to manifest and materialize things of different frequencies into your life. Not only do you have your own vibrational frequency, but you can also manipulate your frequency to vibrate on the same wavelength as the things you would like to attract into your life. You change your vibrational frequency by changing the state of your consciousness. This can work for just about anything money included, and it looks like choosing to operate on the same "level" (vibrate in the same way) as the thing(s) you want.

Without being reductive or weighing down this book/chapter with this teaching, the best way to describe changing your vibrational frequency is to become one with the thing(s) that you want to manifest. You think about it, you operate as if it's already in your life, and you take its structural composition into consideration: what exactly is the thing you want, what are its functions, intrinsic intentions, and capabilities. The key to this, however, is that the thing(s) that you are trying to manifest must come natural to you. You cannot force something to manifest. If it shows up it's because you allowed it to do so and that will only happen if it's a natural feeling, the behavior is not forced, and the desire is true to you.

Essentially, what you put out into the world comes back to you. Humans have the unique ability to drastically influence their lived experience. You can determine your own quality of life. Our emotions determine the type of energy that we effect on to our world.

In the birthday party example that I used in the previous chapter, the man who got upset, his energy casted a negative vibration into that moment. We have all been there before, where something that someone said or did made you or a group of people feel uncomfortable. The energy that we put out affects what the world gives back, and it's our emotions that ultimately determine what we receive. As this relates to respecting money, the reason you want to do so is because whether or not you do or do not will determine how much of it you attract into your life. This is referred to as the Law of Attraction.

The Law of Attraction has a unique effect on money because of the status society places on it. In a way, money in energy form is a collective of will power. You can bend your money to your will. In fact, money is an extension of your will. The Bible says that where our treasure is, our heart is also. Where you put your money is a reflection of what you care about.

Money is not real from a perspective of something worth worshiping however, it is real from the perspective of representing value. I like to think of money as seeds and I am the farmer. Where I shop, how I invest, and what I do with my savings are all representative of plots of land. Each plot has a different type of soil yielding a different level of return. The purpose in sowing your "seeds" in these various plots of land is that you want to extract the most value from your money (seeds) as possible.

When you change your mindset about money you change your perspective on it. No, money is not the root of all evil, but it also will not solve all your problems. Money is an extension of yourself. It's the most effective way in which you impact your life. You can do a whole lot more with money than you can without it; but that is all it is—a resource. The moment you elevate money as something more than that is when you begin to live out of alignment with it. Money is not god, but God uses money.

The best way to improve your relationship with money is to adopt an Abundance Mindset. An Abundance Mindset is a paradigm of thought that says, "I always have everything that I need." When you live in abundance, you live without lack. So, no matter how much or how little of a resource you think you have, whatever it is, it's enough. Living in this way is a choice. You have to choose to say you have enough. You must be willing to objectively examine what you want and whether or not it makes sense for your life. On the flip side of having everything you need, is the inference that you also have nothing that you do not need. This can be likened to living a minimalist lifestyle. Do not live above your means, but also do not live below them; instead, start asking yourself critical questions about your money.

Do you know where every dollar that you bring in goes every month? Do you take advantage of saving opportunities within your monthly expenses as they arise? You may need to have a power shift in relation to your money. While this number is always changing, on average, over half of adults in the United States live paycheck to paycheck. The purpose of money in your life should be for it to work for you, not rule over you.

This is why you need to become the Chief Financial Officer (CFO) of your own life. When money shows up in your life, you need to make sure you are able to tell it where to go as opposed to it telling you where it needs to go. This is why saving, and investing are so important. Bills will always be around—they're the cost of being alive; along with death and taxes. That being the case, however, does not mean you have to submit to working until you are too old to continue to do so, being a ward of your respective state, or just being flat out broke.

By putting money away for yourself you are enacting your will on to your material health. By improving the condition of your finances, you improve the condition of your "material wealth." In the same vein as your material health, your material wealth refers to the quality of things that amalgamate your material health. For most people, the majority of their money goes to things that provide immediate value with no longevity. Think of it like eating food. Every monthly bill represents how much of that resource you consume. At the end of the month, you have to "buy more food" or pay for another month of consumption. While you should want to sustain your quality of life, at some point, your quality of life will have to sustain you. No one works forever. You work hard while you are young so that you can enjoy life when you are older. The only way that will be possible is if you not only sustain for today, but also plan and prepare for tomorrow. If you have not already, you need to plot this course of your life as soon as possible. Write your plans down and make them plain, cast a vision for yourself three, five, and ten years out. Doing so will give you something worth saving for.

How much would you like to make next year? How much money would you like to have saved? How much do you need to retire, and what opportunities would you be open to investing in? What thing(s) do you like that will also retain or appreciate in value? Is buying a house in your near future? You should have a plan for your money- but that will only happen when you have a plan for your life.

THE PURSUIT OF PASSION

The value in saving and investing is that it causes you to put your life in perspective. Remember, your heart is where your treasure is. If you are willing to put your money towards something that will grow over time and will yield you a good return on investment, it says something about your character. To value the importance of saving and investing means that you value a foundational premise of life. It's not about getting as much as you can, it's about maintaining it for as long as you can. The person that is good at handling small amounts will be given authority over more. The person that fails with a little will not be trusted with more. You may have seen this trope play out in life before where you or someone you know wanted a promotion and did not get it, or they thought they were doing a good job at work but was fired seemingly without warning. It's not about the level of responsibility, it's about your ability to handle it. So is the case with money. When you learn to respect it, it will gravitate towards you, and begin to manifest in increasing quantity.

Here are some ways to have a more practical approach with your money that will immediately improve your financial wellbeing:

Pay Yourself First

Every time you get paid you should put away anywhere between 10–30% of what you brought in. Doing this is important because it will redefine your relationship with your money. Most people when they get paid, the first thing that they do is pay their bills. Then they live off of whatever is left over. Paying yourself first flips this pattern. Instead of prioritizing your bills you begin to prioritize yourself. As this pool of money begins to develop over time you can use it as you please whether it's for emergency expenses, investing in the stock market, life insurance, or some other high yielding vehicle; or even occasionally within reason, treating yourself to something nice.

When you place distinct value on your life through your finances, you are subconsciously telling yourself that you matter. Yes, this can be sacrificial however, sacrifice is the cousin of success. You may not be able to get everything you want in life, but you can get life out of everything you have.

Theory is typically easier than practice, and this is no exception to that rule. Based on data gathered in 2022, the average household income in America is around $56,000 a year, while the average household expenditures in America is around $61,000 a year. This means that your average American spends $5,000 more than what they bring in. On top of that, most Americans only have one stream of income. This means that most Americans are in debt. How do you save and invest while living off of a proverbial credit card?

My advice here is to do so anyway. When that paycheck comes in, right in the face of all your bills, pay yourself 30% of your net anyway. Put it in your savings account or take it out in cash. Doing this will do two things that will cause you to look at your situation differently. Firstly, this will cause you to prioritize yourself which will make you see how much you really value your own life. Like do you want to actually improve your life or are you full of it? Secondly, paying yourself first will create the pain necessary for you to want to change your situation if you do in fact care about yourself.

Using the numbers we already have, what this looks like is: your bi-weekly paycheck on a $56,000 salary amounts roughly to $2,333.33. Taxes on this amount of money as a single filer in the United States (most Americans are single filers) is around 22%. After you pay your taxes you are left with roughly $1,820.00. Every month your average expenses come out to $5,083.33. You get paid your net of $1,820.00 every two weeks which adds up to $3,640.00. If that is not painful enough for you already, from that $3,640.00 take out $1,092.00 or 30% for yourself to save for your reinterment, a home, a car, school, paying down debt etc.

The most obvious thing to do would be not pay yourself and use all your money on bills. But that would not solve the $1,443.33 you still need to come up with. This means you are going into some form of debt to cover your average expenses which ultimately is a form of slavery. If you care about not being a slave to money and to your debtors then this should matter to you. On average around 80% of Americans are in debt. Debt and "life, liberty, and the pursuit of happiness," are oxymoronic. You cannot be independent and be a slave at the same time regardless of your nationality. Just ask the African slaves during the slave trade how free they really were.

The best thing to do in the presence of all this pain is to solve it and not just put a band-aid over it. Among other things this looks like paying down debt, reducing expenses, generating income from more than one source, and budgeting.

Create a Budget

Learn to keep track of your money. From this perspective I like to think of myself as a general and my dollars as soldiers. You want to know where every dollar has gone and is going. You may want to include a small margin of error, I like to keep mine between 1-3%, but besides the pennies that may fall through the cracks every dollar should be accounted for.

Categorize your expenses. Break your expenses up into variable and fixed expenses. Your fixed expenses are your monthly bills. These are payments that you know you must pay. Each one should be consistent in cost, and they should come out of your bank account on or around the same day every month. The best thing to do with these expenses is to automate them so you do not have to give too much thought to them.

Your variable expenses are payments that you make or money that you spend on an irregular basis. Examples of these are one-time payments, vacations/excursions, treating yourself etc. You want to keep track of these as well so that you can see what patterns arise in your spending habits. If you find that in a month you are spending too much on something or that you are spending more than you are bringing in, this is where you can begin to make pragmatic changes that will produce long lasting results. Your variable expenses are the heartbeat of your finances; your goal should be to reduce them as much as possible. You do not want to clog up your variable expenses with purchases that you do not need.

Reduce your Spending

After you know what you spend your money on, and your spending habits, this is where you can begin to make tangible life changes. This is also where you may have to ask yourself some difficult questions like: "do I really need to buy a coffee today?" or "is that shirt really worth $35 to me?" Reducing your spending is all about making your dollar stretch. You want to become miserly with your finances.

A successful person says "no" more than they say "yes"; this is because of the value on the proposed opportunity. Everything you do should be valuable. This means that if you absolutely without a shadow of a doubt do not need it, do not get it. Consumerism tells us that the more we have the happier we will be. The only truth about having more stuff is that it takes up more space. The questions you should be asking when looking to reduce expenses are "do I have space for this in my life?" and "Is this thing actually worth the value I would be receiving from it?"

Reducing your spending looks like instead of buying a $5 cup of coffee every day, you purchase coffee grounds and make your own coffee. Or instead of paying $100 for internet, you find a service provider that will offer it to you for $50. Reducing your expenses is not about reducing your overall quality of life, it's about enjoying a full quality of life in a way that is conscious of the ramifications of your decisions—specifically as it relates to your finances.

Your credit is another area of your finances that this touches. When reducing your spending, reducing how much you put on your credit can go a long way. Generally speaking it's recommended to spend no more than 30-40% of your total balance. The best way I heard credit described to me is that it's today you borrowing from future you; and that if you cannot buy it two or three times in cash then you cannot afford to buy it once on credit. Making on time payments on your credit card, carrying a low balance, and having a proper mindset about your spending in general can help you get in front of and take control of your finances in way that will lead to liberation.

Save and invest

From a thematic perspective I have already touched on the value of saving and investing your money. However, from a practical application standpoint there are a few things you should want to do when looking for ways to save and invest.

The first thing you should do is consult your financial professional. Please do not take these suggestions for advice. Let your financial professional help you decide what is best for you. If you do not have one, I suggest getting one that you can trust. After consulting a professional some other things to consider would be the following:

- Setting up a savings account with a high interest rate

- Getting life insurance with a cash value option
- Putting money into the stock market
- Buying assets that will retain or grow in value
- Getting and keeping your credit in good standing
- Creating multiple streams of income (most successful people have at least 3-5 other ways of creating money for themselves outside of their main career)
- Making sure you always have a decent amount of cash on hand in case of an emergency

While this list is not all encompassing it's a good start when looking for ways to preserve your wealth. Your finances are a game of chess not checkers. Be intentional in the decisions that you make, and always do your best to keep future you into consideration when today you wants to do something.

The purpose of all of this is so that you can enjoy the totality of your life. If you do not save enough money on the front end of your life, you will not have any for the latter. And if you spend too much money on the back end of your life, it will not last you very long. Remember, your goal should be to make your money last as long as possible. You do this by putting your money to work—but by doing so strategically.

This being said, do not neglect to treat yourself along the way either. While saving is valuable, so is enjoying your life. There is nothing wrong with taking the trip, buying that new piece of technology, or spending the $5 on the coffee every now and again. Everything should be in moderation—but saving should be ingrained in your lifestyle. Use material items as part of your personal rewards system.

If one month you bring in more money than expected, reward yourself for your hard work, and not because you have more money. Having and keeping money are two different things and should be addressed as such. Have fun when you have the money to do so and enjoy it as a byproduct. Otherwise keep as much of your money as you can for as long as you can.

The last thing that I want to touch on in regard to your finances and your material health and wealth is that you should be looking for active ways to contribute back to society. While your nine to five may be a form of contribution, in reality, working is not selfless in nature. You should be looking for ways to inject value into the world outside of your world.

Helping others, partnering with organizations, and giving back gives you an opportunity to connect with a sense of purpose. It also humbles you in the face of those less fortunate. One of the biggest life experiences to humble me was when I worked in New York. There would always be homeless people on the route to my office and as I would pass them, I would always see me in them.

While I have never been homeless in the sense of living on the streets, I empathize with those people from the perspective of what it must feel like for them to be hungry, or what they may have experienced to land themselves where they are. I would also always take their mental health into consideration and what life must be like for them. Every day that I went into the city, I would be intentional about identifying someone I could potentially help financially or otherwise.

Success is an attitude of gratitude. To whom much is given, much is required. Helping others will help you put and keep that into perspective as you grow in your material wealth. Your money is important. It's part of your overall material health. How you use it and what you think about it will determine the true value that you get from it. Your goal for your money should be to keep as much of it as possible, and the purpose for your money should be for it to be an extension of yourself. Do not be afraid to treat yourself but also remember to pay your success forward. There is always someone less fortunate, and while you may not be able to solve their problem(s), you can acknowledge that you share in their experience via the human condition. All of us are on this planet trying to figure out how to make it. Your money is as good as what you do with it, so learn to deploy it wisely.

Chapter 3

<u>Fitness</u>

The next aspect of your material health that I want to cover is your fitness. Your fitness is about being at peak performance not just physically, but also intellectually, emotionally, and spiritually. This impacts your material health because it's through these aspects of yourself that you engage with the world. From a physical perspective you feel the world around you through your body and your five senses. Intellectually, you have the ability to attain and retain knowledge. You dictate to your environment through your emotions, and you can manipulate your environment with your spirit (will power). As you improve these aspects of yourself, your overall quality of life will improve.

The way in which you become more fit is through training. What are you doing to improve yourself on a daily basis? A question you should be constantly asking yourself is, "am I growing, and if so, how?" Your growth is predicated on your willingness to engage. A person does not get six pack abs simply by thinking about them constantly. They have to put forth the effort necessary to produce abs in their life. You must be willing to put in the work. We live in a world where everything is at our fingertips. In most cases, a person does not have to put too much thought into anything. Technology has gotten so good to the point that before you even have the thought, you are bombarded with a sea of ads about something an algorithm somewhere thinks you might be thinking about. Life is slowly but surely making thinking obsolete. Because of this, people are becoming less and less concerned about "the how" and fixated on "the what." "The what" has become a prized possession in a world of virality and instant gratification. "The how" does not matter as much because if "the how" is too strenuous, people just jump to a different "what." Society has become indoctrinated to desire the benefits of convenience, without fully considering the cost and repercussions thereof. Because of this people are becoming increasingly lazier.

Everyone is becoming a jack of all trades while few are taking the time necessary to master one. Fundamentally, the only way you grow at something is by getting better at it. Growth builds on itself. Most people go to kindergarten before they go to college. Growth is a process that you must be willing to expose yourself to. Laziness is an active choice to not become better. A Lazy person says, I see what could be, and I choose for that to not be for me. As society makes it easier for people to be lazy, people will have a more difficult time finding a reason not to be. As this trend continues to extrapolate across time, success could potentially become a loss art from the perspective of becoming better at something. As a reader of this book that is good news for you, because as you continue to pursue your own personal growth, your intrinsic value will increase over time. As you become better at honing your craft and being yourself, people will inevitably take interest in you. And as people begin to give you attention, opportunities will begin to manifest.

In addition to growth building on itself, it's also nuanced. To be considered an expert at something, a person must put in over 10,000 hours of dedicated time into one specific thing. If you look at a standard learning curve it starts with a steep incline and then begins to level out over time, growing gradually, but at a consistent rate. At the beginning of learning anything new is where you will see the most dramatic growth because typically, that is where the most pertinent information is. Going back to our school analogy, the reason people go to kindergarten first, is because before you can be able to solve a math problem, you need to know what a number is. Before you can color and paint, you need to know what colors are. As you grow in your general knowledge however, you hit a point in the learning curve where, you know just enough to get you through your daily routine. You know how to complete a task without necessarily fully understanding it.

Think of it like buying a computer, tearing it apart, and putting it back together. Most people know how to spend money (in this case for buying a computer), and taking a computer apart is not rocket science. The differentiator in this case would be a person's ability, or lack thereof, to put that computer back together. This is what separates the jack from the master. The master will know how to put that computer back together, while the jack will end up paying the master to do it for them. It pays to be the expert because the expert gets paid. The issue, however, is that it takes more time to become an expert than it does to be a generalist. At this point in the learning curve, your skillset becomes your ability to give attention to the details of your craft. The way you take your life to the next level and begin to see things manifest is by making the details of your life matter. You do this by putting yourself into "Growth Opportunities."

A Growth Opportunity is an environment with the potential to propel you somewhere you have never been before. You must be willing to expose yourself to new experiences. This is about being adaptable. Life is the greatest teacher and sometimes the best way you can learn is by going with the flow. When you are adaptable you can roll with the punches. Allowing your environment to impact your development expands not only your knowledge, but subsequently, your resourcefulness as well. Growth in this case is correlated to your ability to navigate wherever you are. This does not mean when in Rome do as the romans do—what's good for the goose is not always good for the gander; but where you are, should be your training ground. Remember, you want your growth to be perpetual, because if you are not going forward in life, you are not going anywhere.

Every day you wake up, you have the option to get better. You decide whether or not you are going to make a healthy life choice and choose an apple over a cookie. It's up to you to read the entirety of that informative article that is longer than you expected. Meditating, journaling, going to the gym, or going for a walk, are all decisions you get to make in relation to the quality of your own life.

Happiness is a choice and growth is an essential human need. The choices you make in relation to your willingness to grow can have a direct impact on your perceived happiness. People suffer when they feel as though they cannot grow. It's like being claustrophobic and feeling as though the walls are closing in. When you are meant to soar, you cannot go against your nature. That does not mean you begrudge those around you that are not flying with you, instead you come to terms with the fact that eagles tend to fly alone. The inherent feature of being an expert is that not only are you willing to do what others are not, but you are also uniquely capable in doing so. Eagles fly at a higher altitude than most birds simply because they can. Make your strength a strength. What makes you unique is also what makes you better. Do not be afraid to lean into your competitive edge.

The United States in particular has allowed its culture to perpetuate a "Participation Trophy Mindset." The Participation Trophy Mindset says that last place is first place in its own way. Instead of celebrating an obvious victory, people have become more accustomed to cheering on the loser. I use the word loser intentionally because within the context of a competition there is literally only one winner, and either one or a group of losers. While both can be nuanced in their own way, at the end of a sport's game for example, no one ever says that the losing team won too. And even if someone did, that game will reflect as a loss on the losing team's record for that season without debate based on performance and the facts (score) of the game.

I may be biased on this perspective however, I think people need to become more welcoming of competition and specifically, the prospect of losing. Losing at something is good for people because all a loss is, is an opportunity to get better. You learn more from losing than you do from winning. People conflate a loss as a personal defect. People will tend to think that there is something wrong with them when they fail at something or come up short. Society's problem with competition revolves around the value we place on it. Competition is not about making you feel better, it's about proving that you are better.

Becoming a better person in any capacity is the road less traveled. Everyone goes to the gym in January, but by February it's usually a ghost town. Everyone has a personal goal, but only a hand full of people actually achieve theirs. There is a saying that goes, "the graveyard is the richest place on earth because of all the unfulfilled hopes and dreams that it holds." If being competitive and being willing to prove myself means that I get to live a more fulfilling life, then sign me up! I rather compete for first place than settle in last if it means I pushed myself a little more, I gained more knowledge, and I am a better person because of my experience.

It's Time to Get Fit

Improving your fitness looks like taking consistent actions that will compound over time. Choosing to become consistent in the right habits is how you grow physically, intellectually, emotionally, and spiritually. This looks different for everyone, but the same principles apply. You want to make sure that you are constantly being attentive to your needs. This partially stems from your ability to be mindful (of which I will go over in depth in a later chapter); you want to become your own best problem solver.

The first thing you want to look for when growing your material health in this way is whether or not the totality of your being is in homeostasis. Homeostasis refers to a state of equilibrium. Typically, you do not come across this concept outside of an anatomy class however, being at a state of balance and rest does not only apply to your physiology. Before you can begin to improve your life, you must be willing to decipher and deal with the things holding your life back. This looks like addressing the key aspects of yourself and figuring out your status. Are you at peace in your mind, body, spirit, and emotions, or are there things in one or multiple areas of yourself that are causing dissonance?

Rooting out the problem(s) impeding your growth can sometimes be an all-hands-on deck process. Sometimes people decide to tolerate something because they think that it will be easier than if they were to address it directly. The issue with avoidance in this way is, if you give your problem an inch, it will take a mile. The longer you take to address an area of conflict, the more contentious that aspect of your life will become. Eventually, if left unaddressed, what was once benign will have been given room to become malignant.

Problems that have been given time to fester in your life will sprout up new problems. If you find yourself looking at your life and realizing that you have little fires everywhere, the best way to manage them is one at a time. The first step to change is being willing to admit that a change is necessary. By submitting to that process, you will be allowing growth to take place. Once you are finally able to create a sense of peace for yourself, the next thing that you want to be able to do is build on it.

When addressing your fitness, you want your peace to be your foundation. You should be in a state of clarity when making an action plan about your material health. How you meet the needs of your mind, body, spirit, and emotions, should be done in a way that is self-fulfilling and life-bringing. What you do should uplift you and not bog you down. When you are concluding on these types of major decisions, you should want to make sure you are doing so with your best interest in mind. You should also address each aspect of yourself individually. What you need physically will be different than what you need intellectually, which will be different than what you need emotionally, which will be different than what you need spiritually. Addressing each part of yourself individually, will bring to light the specific shortcomings you may have. The solutions that you find for each part of yourself may overlap, but each aspect of yourself should be given special and priority treatment.

An example of this in my life is my gym habit. Working out for me is primarily a physical fitness activity from the perspective of my goal for working out is to improve my physique. The residual effect of me working out however, is that it provides for me a place to release my emotions, clear my head and not overthink, and push myself to be better than my last lift. Working out remedies my physical need to take care of my body, but it also speaks to the other aspects of me that matter too. Within the same context however, even though working out gives me a place to release my emotions, the specific way that I improve that particular area of my life is through reading and writing. So, while a solution for one part of me may ameliorate another, I still engage with an activity or growth action that is tailored to a specific need that may arise within the key aspects of myself.

If you want to start growing, start learning how to fix your problems. Once you know what you need and you have come up with a solution to meet that need, the next and most important thing you want to do is become consistent in your execution. If you decide that the best way to meet the need of your spiritual self for example, is by meditating three times a week for at least 30 minutes, do not expect to constantly achieve your desired result if you only follow your own guidelines for a week and then decide to stop. Consistency means done the same way over time. You must give time, time to play its role in your development. This will only happen when you are adamant and intentional about your actions.

I want to put a caveat here and say, this can be easier said than done. Being consistent can be one of the biggest challenges in life. Consistency can be difficult for a couple of reasons. First and foremost, it's challenging because all of us have a base level of consistency. This is called a habit. All humans have habits. Some habits are good, and some habits are bad. A habit is consistency on auto pilot. These are things that you can do with relative ease because they are things that you have been doing over an extended period of time. A bad habit can be easy to make and hard to break while a good habit, the opposite. Being holistically fit means at the very least having more good habits than bad ones. Another obstacle in a person's consistency can be life. Sometimes life will challenge you by throwing things at you aimed at throwing you off your game. Sometimes life will test you to see how serious you are. If you find yourself coming up against challenges like these it's important to know that consistency is a derivative of itself. You must become consistent at being consistent. Another word for this is persistence. Persistence is the secret sauce-the differentiator between everyone who starts and the ones who finish.

    This it the formula for success: hard work + time x luck. The more effort you put forth over time will be magnified by the opportunities that become available. Success is not just about being in the right place at the right time; it's also about being ready to take advantage of the proper opportunities—and your material health is predicated on your ability to do so. Of your finances, fitness, and future, your fitness may be the most important because if your life is not right, the stuff you have will not matter, and the future you want will not be important. Your overall health and wealth are so intwined together that people do not realize that the only reason they do not have what they want is because they are not growing where it counts. People can have all the money they could want and every future prospect imaginable, but if they are not being intentional in growing and improving every day, then they are not receiving the fullness of their wealth because aspects of themselves are still not healthy.

Take Control of your Imagination

Before I end this chapter, I want to take a moment to lay a foundation around the concept of "spiritual self." I want to target this aspect of you specifically because while most people know what their physical body is and what it can and cannot do, as well as what it feels like to be emotional/have an emotional experience, and to use cognition to produce a thought; people tend to get tripped up on the idea that they are a spiritual being as well and in addition to being sentient in all other aspects of themselves.

Before I dive deeper into Living in Alignment, materializing your material health, achieving your compelling future, and living the life of your dreams, it's important that you understand the role your spirit plays in making all that come to fruition. The three major conflicts that people face are: [genderless] man versus self, man versus nature, and man versus man.

Man versus man is you versus your neighbor in a conflict. Man versus nature is you versus your society and environment. And man versus self is about your internal discourse. When you quarrel with yourself, you are quarreling with your spirit (more is mentioned about this in the "About the Author" section of the book). Have you ever done something that you knew you should not have done, and afterwards, a feeling of guilt consumed you? Or maybe you have been in a place where you were on the precipice of a life changing decision but were too afraid to take a leap of faith. Spiritual conflicts deal with the matters of your heart-the essence of who you are: your personality, the way you communicate, things you like and why you like them etc. All those things stem from your spiritual you. Being intentional in not ignoring this part of yourself for a lot of people is the missing link for their success.

It's not enough to go to the gym regularly, eat ice cream while you cry your eyes out and reflect on your life, or study and learn everything you possibly can. If you are not giving attention to your spirit, you are not living in the fullness of your material wealth. For a lot of people, when they neglect their spiritual self, they tend to feel as though "something is missing." Not making sure your spirit is healthy will leave a noticeable gap in the quality of your life. The thing that people tend to refer to when they say something is missing is purpose. Spirit brings purpose. Your physique, emotional state, and intellect can only contribute but so much to your life without purpose. When your spirit is on par with the rest of you that means there are no gaps and that your fitness needs are being met. When this is happening in your life, you give yourself license to be creative.

Creativity is the secret ingredient of life. It's the pancetta in the carbonara, the skill in the technique, and the finesse in the finish. All of us have desires. The word "De-Sire" in Latin literally means "Of the Father." Your desires are sown and germinated in your spirit before they sprout forth materially. The first encounters we have with our desires start in our imagination. Your imagination is primarily dependent on your creative ability. When you imagine your desires, you are creating an alternative reality. By engaging with what could be you dissociate from what actually is, even if only for a moment. When you incorporate the other three aspects of your fitness into this process, you begin to direct your life energy (vibrations) towards what you are envisioning. And when your vibrations are in alignment with the vibrations of what you want, then the Law of Attraction kicks in and now you are actively manifesting a compelling future for yourself. I will cover the gap between manifestation and materialization later but essentially, this is the process of being able to walk before you can run. Where are you going if you do not know where you are going? I can personally say that I have not, nor do I know anyone who has booked a flight to nowhere. What shows up in your life only does so because you invite it to. You only receive what you believe you are worthy of receiving. If you do not see yourself having, being, or doing anything, then you will not.

Your imagination allows you to see what could be. This is called suspending your unbelief. The problem is people tend to only use their imagination to exacerbate what already is. If you could think back to when you were a child, what would you do to entertain yourself? When I was growing up my sister and I would play "don't touch the lava," where we would jump around to different designated "safe" areas on the floor and avoid touching the lava (areas considered not safe). Was there actually lava there? No. Was it fun? Yes! Another thing I would do growing up is imagine all the cool superpowers that I wanted. For me still to this day my number one favorite superpower is teleportation/super speed. I do not know if it was the same for you, but as a kid, I had all the time in the world to imagine how great my world could be. As we grow older however, our youthful awe and wonder turns into, fear and skepticism. Before I knew it, I went from flying on the backs of imaginary dragons to being anxious about whether or not I would get approved for a loan. The problem is we allow our reality to co-op our imagination. You cannot see something new, different, or exciting because you know too much about your own problems. Instead of being someone who can only complain about what is, try being someone who can imagine what could be.

Chapter 4

Future

What is a vision? I have alluded to this concept before, but now I want to take a deeper dive into what it means. A vision is when you have something to hope for. A vision is different from a dream because a dream can be fleeting. You can dream about something today and something else tomorrow, a vision however, has an element of consistency. It's something that you know you want. A vision is rooted in your desires. For example, if you desire to get married, then it's likely you to have a vision for what you would want your marriage to look like. If you have a desire for a pet as another example, then you probably have an idea of what kind of pet you would like. Your vision informs your desires because you cannot appreciate what you cannot recognize. The Bible says that without vision the people perish. Vision gives life to your desires and your desires give light to your life.

Another word you can use for desires is "hope." Your vision is a transcription of your hope. It helps you see what it is that you want. If you do not want anything (desire/hope) then you will not try to get anything (have vision) which ultimately means you will not have anything (perish). It's in the trying to achieve that your hope gets put into action. I have hope that this book does well; and it's my hope that causes me to put forth the degree of faith and effort necessary to write, publish, and market. This is why knowing what you want is so important—because what you want will dictate where you go. Think of it like different career paths. Most people want to be able to make a living for themselves. The way in which each person decides to do that, however, can be dynamically different. Whether you are a Stockbroker or a Librarian, where you are in life is a byproduct of where you see yourself going.

People lose vision because they get comfortable. Another word for this is settling. Settling is not inherently a bad thing. At a certain point we all should extract a certain amount of comfortability out of life. Most people, however, have a tendency of settling too soon and in the "wrong" areas of their life. To settle means to devalue yourself. When you willingly accept what is/wherever you are in life, you put a cap on your growth. It's like a running faucet. While the water is running, that is a representation of you growing and developing. When you turn the water off, that is a representation of you deciding you are done (settling). The latent issue with this is, when you put a proverbial cap on your life, you do not know what you are missing out on by deciding not to continue. You must know your worth. You only receive what you believe you are worthy of receiving. When you stop having vision for your life, you allow death to start taking root. Consider a home. You know a house has life in it because lights are on, its clean, and the grounds are being up kept. You know a house is dying or dead because probably no one lives or has lived there for some time, there may be roots and weeds growing all over the property, and its foundation is possibly eroded. So is the case with our lives when we allow ourselves to depreciate in value. By choosing not to grow and to settle in a place you were only meant to visit, you deprive yourself the fullness of your compelling future.

It's called a compelling future because it's supposed to be a future that draws you closer to it. Your future should have a strong magnetic pull. It should be so encapsulating that until you get there, nothing else could ever or would ever measure up.

Your future is an important part of your material health because without knowing where you are going you will not be able to effectively manage where you are. What's the purpose of financial wealth if you do not know what you want to do with it? Remember, your money is only as good as how you use it. What is so great about being physically, intellectually, emotionally, and spiritually fit, if you do not stay inspired? Your future speaks to these areas of your life and tells them where they should be going. Your future says that based on your desires and the vision that you have for them, these are the things that you should be doing with your fitness and finances to ensure that you are in the best possible position to achieve the next nearest goal. Success is a step-by-step process.

You do not just go from nothing to something overnight. There is a path that has led you to where you are, and one that leads you to where you are going. Success is a trail, and that trail has obstacles. The essence of your future material health is in whether or not you are willing to choose to be happy every day. Perpetual happiness is comparable to joy. You should want to live in a way where every day brings you joy. When you have vision, you are willing to push forward because you have a hope that today will be better than yesterday. Even if yesterday was a good day in and of itself.

Success is Subjective and Potential does not Mean Anything

Your future material health is unique because it's yours. What you choose to want for yourself may be different than what someone else may choose to want for themselves. Your desires would not have been given to you if they were not meant to be fulfilled through you.

Stop worrying about how green someone else's grass is. Their grass is as green as they want it to be. Is your grass as green as you want it to be? If it is, then you do not have time to concern yourself with someone else's. People will see other people's lives and the "amazing" things they are doing and get so caught up in how nice something looks, without even realizing what it took to make that something look nice in the first place. Before a cake becomes a cake its flour. A stage has to be put together; and raw materials have to be gathered before a house can be built. You must work before you receive a paycheck. Your success is a byproduct of your work, and your work is subjective of what you want. I am not going to work for a yacht if I do not like being on boats (which I do not). You are not going to try to materialize something that you do not want—and if you do, you will be/are living out of alignment with yourself.

Before you gawk over someone else's glory, make sure you know their story. When you know what someone else has been through, what they have may not seem so significant. Their grass is only that vibrant because they bought the super expensive high-end mulch. Do you want to carry the burden of dealing with high end mulch? And even if you have it, it will be no good if you are unwilling to work with it. What you have is only as good as the value you extract from it. The word potential literally means nothing.

To have potential means to have or show the capacity to become or develop into something in the future. Your potential is what you could be or what you could have. The only thing is people could have and be a lot. An undirected potential is an unfulfilled future. If you do not set a course for yourself, you will not end up going anywhere. Your future material health is essential to your overall material wealth because with it you have the potential to make an impact that is transcendent. How you dictate your future will affect how someone else will dictate theirs. What if you are meant to be a trail blazer and a trend setter? It will not happen if you do not realize the totality of your desires. In a way, not realizing your compelling future is inherently selfish. By choosing not to be the best version of yourself possible at all stages of your life you are depriving others the opportunity to benefit from your success.

The thing you need to understand is, that the only way any of this works is if you have a vision for your future that is big enough to include others. The moment you lose your ability to give back to others is the moment you lose your worth in the marketplace of life. People only go in one of two directions: forward and nowhere. When you do not have a future, you are not going anywhere. If you are not going anywhere that means you are waiting to die. If you do not get anything else from this book get this: do not wait for death, it's going to show up for you whether you are waiting for it or not. Make your life worth something by making it be for someone else. That is the true value of your future material health, your legacy.

When this thing called life is all said and done what is it that you will want to have been known for? People do not like looking towards the future because they do not like thinking about their death. The problem is, by trying to avoid your mortality you are denying yourself the opportunity to be mortal. You could die before you finish reading this sentence... did you? Hopefully not. Not to get awkward but to prove a point, if you want your death to be less scary start thinking about your future. Everyone's future is death, but before you die what are you going to do? And what will you have done that will have outlived you?

This is what true success is really about, creating something that will continue what you started. What that looks like is subject to be different for everyone however, how it manifests is not as important as the fact that it does. Each one of us has a mandate on our lives to go forth and multiply in a way that is unique to us. Your multiplication should have your mark. How will someone know that you were here? When you are long gone what will bare your resemblance?

This is what your future material health is all about. In conjunction with your finances and your fitness, when these three aspects of yourself come together in harmony, you are officially Living in Alignment. When you are Living in Alignment you are in position for the miraculous to take place in your life. When you are aligned the totality of your being goes in the same direction, and when this happens your world around you will begin to conform to the world inside of you. When you live in alignment every day you manifest your compelling future and materialize into your reality the desires of your heart. Pursuing what you are passionate about is about pursuing what drives you. If your desires are not driving you that means you are dying. Your desires can and will propel you into new life when you have a vision for them that includes other people. If you do not have a hope for your future, you will inevitably have no future to hope for. The first step to sequencing your life for success is figuring out where you are, and where you are going. And where you go only matters if you have a reason to go there.

Chapter 5

Living in Alignment

You are a spiritual being having a physical experience. I am going to be drilling this point into your head throughout the duration of this book because without understanding that the rest of this just will not make sense. This has nothing to do with religion. The God you worship is your choice, what I want you to understand however is, that regardless of intentionality, we live in a world where what you do has ripple effects and can impact those around you. There are universal laws like the Law of Vibration, the Law of Attraction, and the Law of Reciprocity. These are the ways in which the world around us just naturally works: everything moves, like things attract, and you get what you give. These are on par with gravity-what goes up, must come down-they are time tested facts to how the world works.

There are also subrules that operate in the lives of the individual that the universe recognizes and rewards because of one's obedience. Think do unto others as you would have others do unto you, or the principle of giving to receive, or the Law of Value which states that you are only as valuable as how much value you provide to others. These laws and others frame our daily lives. When we do something in our material worlds a ripple gets set off in the spiritual world. The energy that we put out gets enacted upon by the universal laws and based on the degree at which our will is willing to abide by the will of the universe for us, what we put forth will be reflected in what we receive.

What I am trying to say here is this: the culmination of your life, and the quality thereof, is predicated on how you choose [or not choose] to interact with the world around you. this can be boiled down to everyday decisions. What you do on a daily basis has future consequences. Do you live with future you in mind?

Repetition is the mother of learning. As you continue reading, ideas and principles will resurface throughout the subsequent paragraphs and chapters. The purpose of this is so those ideas and principles can begin to penetrate and ingrain themselves in your mind and thought process.

A common practice among most if not all successful people is casting a vision. Where are you going if you have nowhere to go? The Bible says that faith without works is dead. Well works without faith is nonsensical. Who gets up every day just to be up?

We all have an inherent hope for something. The word desire means "Of the Father." The implication of this is the things that you long for were actually pre-programed in you. Consider a new phone. When you purchase a phone, the first thing that you will notice after starting it and setting it up, is that there are several applications already installed on the phone—often which cannot be deleted. In the same way, we all have goals or things that we want, that stick with us until and even after they are satisfied. Consider the condition of the curious cat. The only thing that allowed it to live again was satisfaction. Some people die from a lack of satisfaction.

As I write this book and chapter in real time, I am thinking about what inspired me to do so. My life's journey to this point has been arduous. Trial after struggle after hardship after heartbreak time and time again. Through it all though, writing has never not been present. The first journal I ever had was in middle school, and it opened me to a world of bliss. Whatever I have needed my writing to be through the years, that's what it has become. Whether it be a speech/presentation, research report, published articles, blog posts, a book, my therapist, my friend, my entertainment etc. Does what you do satisfy you, and if so, how? If your answer to that question is "no" or "yes for the purpose of money [or some other material aspiration]," then you are not living in a way that best represents who you really are.

I had a friend for example who was obsessed with money. Now, there is nothing wrong with money, this book has a whole comprehensive chapter about it. I even used to be a financial planner. I have a desire to be able to live and take care of myself just like anyone else; and one of the motivating factors for this book was the prospect of making money. However, the person being referred to talked about money in a way that denoted worship.

This is a dishearteningly common practice around the world where a good portion of people worship at the altar of the almighty dollar. The issue with that is money does not have any intrinsic value. All money is, is an enabler. It enables you to be more or less of who you already are. It itself does not change you. You may change because of it, but other than being a tool that allows you to do "stuff," money is a made-up concept imagined by governments to keep people polarized and socially dependent. When you die, even if you burry your money and possessions with you, those things will be of no use to you. Man made money. Your money will not be with you on the other side of the grave. It's a real simple concept that people for whatever reason get tripped up on.

Ask yourself this, do you know any real-life dead people? Not metaphorically dead, but rather a stereotypical zombie like person, who orders food and rides in a car like a fully alive person. I personally do not know anyone like this. People who do not have oxygen flowing through their lungs do not and cannot consume things like living human beings. This argument can come off as trivial especially to the "God/afterlife is not real" people reading this; however, I would argue purely from a factual, actual, and pragmatic perspective that regardless of your thoughts on those abstract concepts the fact remains that your default setting is not to pursue money.

Monetary idolatry is not something that you are necessarily born into from a genotypical perspective. It's something that you are taught/grow into. Somewhere during the course of my friend's life, he was influenced to believe to some degree that money was satisfactory to and for his purposes in life. I am not knocking his or your life choices, I just want to help you think differently about things. Consider an unhappy rich person. Why are they unhappy with all the money they could ever have, want, and need? Here is the truth, money will never satisfy the you inside of you.

Going back to our phone analogy, depending on the type of phone you have, every few months you may receive an alert on your phone to conduct a software update. This update is essential because it reduces bugs and glitches, provides an upgrade to the existing software, and helps with the phone's overall performance and battery consumption. Money is a proverbial hardware update. With money you can change the container, but you cannot change what is inside of it. To be who you were always meant to be, to satisfy your desires, and to be as successful and effective as possible, you need a software update not a hardware update.

What good is a new laptop running an old operating system? What good is all the money in the world if you have not taken the time to do the inner work necessary to promote a fulfilling life. Works without faith is senseless—and money and material things without personal awareness is pointless.

Being a spiritual being means that you have the power to actualize (manifest) the world around you. The Law of Attraction, which operates under the law of vibration, allows for you to "magnetically" pull into your life essentially whatever you want. The idea is that by changing your vibrational frequency through your emotional state you can vibrate at the same frequency as your wants and desires.

Money has its own frequency, cars have their own frequency, houses have their own frequency, even vacation destinations have their own frequencies. Anything in physical form, meaning you can taste, touch, smell, see, or hear it, has its own vibrational frequency. As a human being you have the power to change the frequency that you put out into the world. The type of frequency that you release (the level at which you vibrate on) determines what comes into your life (what you attract). Think of it like switching lanes on a highway. Depending on the lane that you are in, that will subsequently inform how fast you wind up driving. In the same way, depending on your vibrational frequency, that will subsequently inform what you end up attracting into your life.

This is key to understand when trying to live in alignment and manifest the life that you want. You only get out of this life what you believe you are worthy of receiving. Life withholds nothing from us, but we withhold life from ourselves. This is why knowing what you want is so important. Before you can bring to fruition the desires of your heart, you first must be able to articulate what those desires are. This comes from having a vision.

This is where the pursuit of passion starts— by understanding what you are passionate about, and then figuring out how to pursue it. This is also why it's important to have a clear understanding of the things that you value in your life, otherwise you could end up pursuing the wrong things. Understanding that you are a spiritual being also means that you realize that your purpose is greater than your stuff.

For you to have an effective vision you must have one that includes others. The reason why you want a vision that can include others is because then that vision will be big enough to include you. People can have a tendency to be too narrow minded. They think that things can only happen in a certain way and for only certain people. Miracles are normal, and they can happen for you too. But in order for you to have a life changing experience, you have to be able to identify something in your life that needs to change.

Innovators find better ways to do the same thing. Before computers there were typewriters and before cars there were horses and carriages. The problem never changed, needing to prepare a formal writing, or having to travel from one place to another; the solution to that problem just got better. As is the case with almost anything, too much innovation can be a bad thing and does require moderation however, you have the right to innovate your life.

As a creator you have the right to say that you want to fix or change something for the better. The key to your success in this area is having a motivating factor that will sustain itself pass its own fulfillment. Whatever it is that pushes you to want to be successful, live passionately, and receive all that this life has for you, must be big enough and strong enough to endure being accomplished. What I mean is, what happens after you buy the house? You've wanted a new car for so long, what happens after you get it? That degree that you worked so hard for, what happens after you get it and enter an unforgiving and uncompassionate job market?

Having a vision that is large enough to include others means that it's large enough to include you because it will give your purpose room to flourish. Your purpose goes beyond what you do, it's rooted in who you are. This is why it's important to detach yourself from things that are misrepresentative to who you are. This is about knowing yourself. The pursuit of passion at its core is self-actualization, but you cannot actualize what you cannot identify. Have you ever taken the time to ask yourself, "who am I?" Who are you with everything stripped away? No bells, no whistles, no status, no clout; just you barebones and by yourself; who are you?

That is a heavy question, and one we tend not to like to ask ourselves however, that is the question that stands in the way between who you currently are and who you could potentially become. Somewhere in the response to that question is your sentiment towards your neighbor. When you ask yourself who you are, you are also subconsciously asking yourself how you feel about your fellow human. This is important because no one is an island unto themselves. The larger the vision the greater the degree of influence.

That does not mean that only influential people can dream, but rather the opposite, everyday regular people can have influence. This is the proverbial graveyard of dead dreams—a lack of influence. This is why legacy is so important and why this process as a whole is so effective because the whole thing is cyclical. By learning how to live in alignment, you can orchestrate your life in such a way that it plays out right before you. Instead of striving, you will be living with an expectation. Once you develop this process in your own life, it becomes a default setting. Having vision, casting direction, executing a plan, and believing for better (looking for new ways to innovate), will become second nature to you once you start Living in Alignment. Having this level of structure is key to sequencing your life for success.

How to Live in Alignment

With this understanding of the importance of the process I can begin to extrapolate on what the process itself looks like. Sequencing your life—Living in Alignment, starts with fidelity to yourself. That is the frame from which we can begin to paint this picture. It's paramount that you are committed to yourself when setting out to change your lifestyle; because they that do not stand for anything will fall for everything. You should have some base level convictions and confidence in who you are. It's always of your prerogative to change your mind however, that should be a 100% educated and autonomous decision especially in the case of how you conduct your life. Do not be wishy washy. When you know who you are you will not flirt with who you are not. Double mindedness leads to dissonance and inner conflict. The Bible says that one cannot serve two masters.

The first step to Living in Alignment is to have something to look forward to. After reaffirming your core principles there should be a point in that process where you discover or rediscover your desires. These are things that you know that you want. These wants live in your heart and in your soul. They are usually extravagant in their own way, and when you think about them, they bring to you/produce a sense of peace, brief as it may be. That is your compelling future. That is the thing that gets you up in the morning whether it be consciously or subconsciously. That is the motivating factor that will outlive its own fulfillment. Once you know what that is, you now have something to look forward to. This one piece is so important it will influence the rest of this process until you start it again.

    The second step to Living in Alignment is to exert your freedom of choice. Now that you know where you are going, the next thing for you to do is to decide how you are going to get there. This is where you can allow your creativity to mold your destiny. How you get to where you are going is just as if not more important than your arrival. We all are on a journey to somewhere, your job is to make sure that, that somewhere is not nowhere. In life, nowhere is a location. It's home to being too small in stature, its where dead dreams go to roost, and where same old stays same and old. If you do not do anything else with your life, make sure you leave that place. Death looks for you where you are "supposed to be" or "used to be" before it looks for where you are now. In other words, do not hinder

THE PURSUIT OF PASSION

your progress because of a lack of ambition. If you think it, you can become it.

Exerting your freedom of choice means setting a course to your destiny that reflects-looks like the you imbodying (living in) your compelling future. Who is the you that you see doing the things that you today wish you could be doing? That you is the real you, and that is the person that you want to be manifesting. People try so hard to manifest things, well, the inverse to that is, things are looking for who is manifesting them. In the most basic of terms, you cannot attract stuff that is not attracted to you. Your gravitational pull is in who you are. Imbody what you want until what you want becomes your reality. Success leaves trails, and every person who is of notable success in a given field or industry "looks" like what they do. This is not always literal even though a businessperson does in fact have a different uniform than a chef or astronaut, but in a lot of ways this is allegorical. Do you speak the language of who you want to become? Do you know the vernacular of your future?

There is a saying that can sometimes have a negative connotation that goes "those who cannot do, teach." I would argue that the value of being able to teach is that you know. Do you know what it takes to become who you want to be? Before you attempt it, do you know it? I cannot begin to tell you how many times I took a job not knowing what was fully required of me, or what I was stepping into. I would encourage you not to do this with your future, it's far too valuable. The problem with not studying and knowing what you may be getting yourself into while in pursuit of your passion is that you will be wasting your time. Passion only costs time but your time on earth is finite. The better you know yourself and the you in your compelling future, the less time you will waste trying and doing things that are misrepresentative of who you really are.

Step three to Living in Alignment is creating a regimen–starting your journey. After seeing where you want to go and figuring out a way to get there, the next thing to do is to execute on your vision. This is where your works come in. You have already demonstrated to yourself that you have faith enough to believe for something that matters to you regardless of how vague it is; so now, the only logical next step is to act on that faith. And the best way to do that, is by having [developing] a regimen around your compelling future. This is not a one size fits all kind of deal, and it's subject to change as your life changes however, you need to have something in place that not only progresses you through your day (meaning getting you from the time you wake up, to when it's time for you to go back to sleep), but also brings you closer to your desires.

In some extreme cases, this can and does look like forgoing sleep to bring to fruition your purpose. When I worked a traditional 9-5 job after I would get off and do my homework (left over work from the day that I did not complete in the office), that is when I would consider that my day had officially started. If what you do is not advancing your compelling future by bringing it closer to becoming a reality, then do not consider it as part of who you are. My job at that time was for the primary purpose of supporting my lifestyle, but my lifestyle was not what was supporting inner me. It's important to measure what matters when working towards Living in Alignment. As such, because I was not only trying to survive, but thrive as well, I would work for myself after I finished working for my stuff. You need to have a regimen in place that is in support of, and adaptable to your current lived experience. One way you can do this, is by having an anchor activity or activities.

An Anchor activity is something that you would do as part of your regimen that denotes either the end of one cycle of events, or the beginning of another. Consider these activities as bumper rails to your life. Not all of these should or have to be daily, but they should be frequent enough to signal to your mind that you are at a certain point in your current alignment regimen. These anchor activities could be comprised of anything. Mine typically include making my bed, washing the dishes, showering, playing video games, and meditating. Regardless of what I do in between those activities, when it's time for me to do one of the aforementioned, it indicates to me that I am at a certain point in my regimen. Anchor activities are like video game checkpoints—based on where you end up it should inform where you go next.

The fourth and final step to Living in Alignment is to assess your progress. Once you have discovered what you desire (had a vision), made a plan around achieving it, and have put that plan into action on a daily basis, the last thing for you to do is to make sure that plan is working. It's important that in this step you give yourself some grace and mercy. Everyone could always be doing more but Living in Alignment means being productive and not just busy. Are you doing what is required for you to achieve the level of success that you want, or are you doing stuff just for the sake of doing stuff? Some people like being busy just so that they can complain about how busy they are. That's all fine and dandy however, how is you being busy helping you to achieve your purposes?

When you assess your progress, you must be honest with yourself. Are you really getting better? And if so, how? Are you closer to your compelling future today than when you first started your alignment journey? To ensure that you are getting the most out of your life today and not 10 years from now, and to understand the effectiveness of your plan, what you are doing today should represent who you really are for the purpose of developing who you desire to become. Video games are part of my regimen because I like playing video games. No, I do not play them like I used to, but playing video games today is an essential part of who I become tomorrow (metaphorically not necessarily literally) if for no other reason than it teaches me to keep and incorporate down time as part of my life. I am always going to want to have down time. That may not look like playing video games at a point—but I will cross that bridge if I get there. The fact of the matter is who you become in your compelling future is predicated on who you are today. You know your plan is effective if it represents all three phases of your life: past you, present you, and future you.

Past you is who you have always been. This is referring to your essence, the things that make you unique and make you stand out in a crowd. Present you is a mash up of what you have lived through and what you are currently living through, and how you consciously manage that experience. Future you is the you, you look forward to. An effective plan takes all three into account. This is why self-confidence and living with fidelity to yourself is a prerequisite to Living in Alignment, because if you are not doing what matters to you, how can you become all that you are meant to be? The world teaches us assimilation, while our spirits command us to individuate. The less of someone or something else that you become, the more of yourself you become. You must know you.

Consider a plant. All plants are not the same. They are all plants meaning part of the Plantae Kingdom however, an equisetum is not a lycopodium, which is not a gymnosperm. They all need different living conditions to be fruitful (no pun intended) and reach their potential. In the same way, for you to be all that you are called to be—achieve whatever it is the father has put in you, you need to be in the proper living conditions. Alignment is not just doing all the time, it's also being. How effective is your plan at helping you just be? If you died tomorrow having never reached your compelling future, will you have been content with how close you got to it? This is the true value of Living in Alignment and what the Bible refers to as the secret of life—living in contentment.

Regardless of where you are going, are you satisfied with the vehicle taking you there? Not everyone is comfortable doing a cross country trip in a hooptie. And doing a cross country trip in the newest model year SUV can be expensive. Is your vehicle-your plan-right for you, or do you need to trade it in and change it? That is the purpose of assessment and evaluation in this process; to find out not only if what you are doing is working, but also if whether or not it's the best way in your current phase of life to get you to your compelling future. Everyone's journey is different, but the important thing is not how you get to your destination, but that you get to your destination... or at least die trying.

Those are the four steps to Living in Alignment—sequencing your life for success. Now, let me be perfectly clear, this is admittedly not an easy process. From having a vision, to creating and executing a plan, to make it a reality takes a lot and frankly is not for the faint of heart. This is the road less traveled. Some people get stuck at step one. What do you do when you do not have a vision? Create one for yourself. But what if you cannot even do that? What does that look like and how does one overcome it? When you start creating your plan how far ahead should you plan? How do you know that what you are doing is going to work in the first place? What do you do when it seems like you are doing all that you know how to do to no avail? And what is this whole living in contentment thing about; how do you do that and are you doing it right now? How successful is successful and when will you know that you have "made it?" All these questions and more are in the details of Living in Alignment. This is where we get into the weeds of this process, and why a lot of people will not be/are not up for the journey.

The rest of this book talks about what that journey looks like. I am going to show you what it looks like to make it to your unassailable end. By the time you finish reading this book you will have a full understanding of what the journey/process of Living in Alignment looks like, and the value thereof in totality. I find this method of living to be the most effective way to directly impact your material wealth. Like things attract, you cannot proclaim royalty while living debased. You cannot declare you are rich while hemorrhaging money. And you cannot achieve the desires of your heart if you do not become what is required of you to do so. Living in Alignment solves the dead dreams problem because before you even take a step you have to dream. And solving the dead dream problem means having influence, and influence confesses success. When you live in a way that influences those around you, while staying committed and true to who you are, that is how you achieve contentment through alignment, and how you make your dreams a reality.

Chapter 6

The Power of a Breakthrough

$\mathcal{T}$he purpose of Living in Alignment, and the effectiveness of it, is in its ability to usher you up to the point of a breakthrough. A breakthrough is a moment where the stars align so to speak. It's a Kairos moment. It's when the table is set, everything is in place and the "show" can start. In stock market terms a breakthrough is a "gap up." It's when what was once holding you back moves out of your way. A breakthrough is the difference between living in mediocrity and realizing the potential of your possibility. This is important because a breakthrough changes everything. I could end this chapter right here, because with that amount of information, you have enough to change the trajectory of your life.

A lot of people like to say that they are waiting for a breakthrough when in reality, your breakthrough is waiting for you. In the Bible there is this story about a man who could not walk for 38 years. He was lame; however, his breakthrough was right in front of him. In the story of this man's life, we are told that he was placed near a pool in his hometown that had the power to allow him to walk again. For years he sat by this pool and never got in it; all the while, his family, friends, and neighbors could not wait to get in it themselves. And presumably, because of human nature, I am sure he (the lame man) saw several of the same people show up, time and time again. This is how breakthroughs function in our lives. It's not enough that a breakthrough shows up, you also have to be in a position to receive it.

This man could not handle the reality of him potentially being able to walk. In the same way, some people cannot handle the reality of the potential of them being able to get, be, and do, better. A breakthrough does for us what the character of Jesus eventually does for that lame man—offer an opportunity to get better. This is where innovation meets progress, where creativity meets a blank canvas, and where raw materials meet a blueprint. This is important because if you were to be honest with yourself for a moment, sometimes you may not know what to do. When you came into this world, you did not come with a manual.

Consider self-assemble furniture. When you buy the piece and or set you want, and get it into your home, you still have to put it together; typically, by following the instructions that it comes with. Unlike furniture, after you were born you still needed to be "assembled," but there were no instructions on how to do so. A breakthrough helps us by giving us direction. Parents get better at raising their children over time because they are constant recipients of revelation about them. The more they learned about their children, the better they become at understanding and subsequently engaging with them. That is a breakthrough.

If your vision is the destination, and Living in Alignment the vehicle, then a breakthrough is your road map. It will show you the way to where you are going. So, the question then becomes how do you know when you are on the verge of a breakthrough? The answer is that you do not and will not know. Breakthroughs are unexpected. You will not know one has shown up until it is either already happening or has passed you by. It's key here for me to take a moment to explain the characteristics of a breakthrough.

A breakthrough is unique in that it's not a miracle (specially natural or significantly normal), but it also is not uncommon. Breakthroughs are both rare and common at the same time. Not normal, but not abnormal either. To use a food analogy, they're like wagyu beef. Wagyu is a breed of Japanese cattle that produces one of the if not the finest cut of red meat a cow could offer. The significance of a cut of wagyu is in its fat marbling. When cooked properly a wagyu steak is like butter in meat form. The draw back to this decadency, however, is that it can be expensive and sometimes hard to find. Wagyu beef is no different in form from any other beef producing cow, the difference is in its luxuriousness. A breakthrough simply put, is a luxurious opportunity.

An opportunity is a "chance"–something for you to take advantage of. You come across opportunities every day in various forms. They are favorable circumstances for you to enact your ambitions on for the purpose of flourishing and benefiting your needs, wants, and desires. They are common. An opportunity is a dime a dozen. You do not have to look too far for a moment that could potentially get you ahead in some area of your life. When you see a person that you are attracted to, that is an opportunity to grow in your love life. When you are looking for a job, you are looking for an opportunity to impact your career and or financial wellbeing. Going to the gym is an opportunity to improve your physical health and your overall quality of life. Opportunity is always all around us.

A breakthrough, however, is an unforeseen opportunity. It's a sudden change. A breakthrough looks like the promotion you were not expecting, the extra money you came into that you were not planning for, or the blind date that your friend sets you up on that actually goes well. It's the thing that changes everything. It's what you know you need but do not anticipate will show up.

What makes a breakthrough so much different than an opportunity, aside from its rarity, is its impact. A breakthrough is an opportunity on steroids as it relates to its ability to thrust you into a new dimension. A good breakthrough can literally change your life forever. With a good breakthrough, you can go from not knowing how to make ends meet, to helping others make their ends meet. A good breakthrough can take you from the back of the room to center stage in a matter of mere moments. These are the moments that Living in Alignment helps you orchestrate your life around. You may not know the size of your breakthrough, when it's going to show up, or how impactful it might be, but if you are Living in Alignment, when it does eventually show up, you will be ready.

The value of being ready is truly beyond comprehension. The Bible states that a person should always be ready. Ready for what you ask? Whatever it is you need to be ready for. Whatever is in your life, that is what you need to be prepared to dominate at all levels. If your boss called you in to give a big presentation to his boss and other important figures in your company, would you be ready? A third string player on a football team may not see the field during a big game however, if enough key players get hurt, that third string player will immediately be propelled to first string; it will have been his job in that moment to have been ready. When you live in alignment, readiness is your superpower. It's your spider sense, your x-ray vision, and your telepathic abilities.

Chapter 7

Who are You?

Who do you say that you are? The words that you use matter. The most important person that you will ever speak to is yourself. Your opinion of you matters more than the perception others have of you. it's one thing for someone else to say something negative about you, it's another for you to say something negative about yourself. The Bible tells us that life and death are in the power of the tongue; what you speak reverberates. Repetition is the mother of learning. This is important to understand because once you do you realize that what you recite you receive.

To receive something means that it takes up residence in your mind. To receive a thought or a word spoken to, about, or around you, is to after hearing it, spend time meditating on it. We all dwell on things. Some things we dwell on longer than we should. And sometimes we dwell on stuff that we should have never been exposed to in the first place.

I grew up in a not so friendly family environment. There was a misconception on the concept of love that prevented me from fully latching on to whatever sense of nurturing I was provided. As a result, I am a loner. My mother passed away when I was five years old. From that moment on, it was a hodgepodge of adults (kids who were older than me) trying to put the missing pieces together to a puzzle they were unfamiliar with. At this point in my life, I do not blame anyone for what they did or did not do however, I cannot deny, and it's possible you may be able to relate to the fact, that sometimes a perceived negative experience can linger in your mind.

That is called trauma. When something jarring from your past gets triggered (brought to the forefront of your mind) in the present. If/when that happens it can cause you to revert to your primal survival tactics that you developed from when that trauma was initially present in your life. I am not suggesting that everything you or I have been through in our childhood is traumatic and therefore has left a negative imprint. We all have different backgrounds however, you joining me on this book journey partly implies that you want more from life than what it has offered you thus far.

Part of understanding your harvest is knowing what has been planted. Be careful of who you allow to tend to the proverbial garden of your life. You may have things cropping up in your life that are designed to inhibit your growth simply because of one thing that someone older than you said that took root when you were young and has now become an obstacle and a stumbling block.

How do you clear the pathway to your destiny? You must clear out what is not supposed to be there; and this in part is done by changing the way that you speak to yourself. The problem with speaking better, is that it does have a prerequisite.

To "speak life," life has to already be in you. From the tongue resounds the overflow of your heart. What you believe you speak. If you are struggling with speaking better, it's because you are not believing better. Once you comprehend this, everything else in this book will start to make a lot more sense. What does it mean to believe better?

Well, let's look at our current process as laid out in the previous chapters for attaining the degree of success awaiting you in your life. First you have a vision—a distant goal, then you get your life in alignment—manage your material life to the point of, finally, having a breakthrough that propels you closer to your vision and goal. Vision, Alignment, Breakthrough, these are the three core competencies of creating the life that you want. The foundation on which these three things stand is belief. What you believe will determine what you envision. What you envision will influence the effort you put forth towards what you see. And the effort you put forth, will manifest itself through the opportunities that become made available to you. Simply put, you have not because you want not.

It's okay to not want more for yourself but that has to be a conscious decision. Do not let things and circumstances rob you of choice. When that happens, that is the will of a nefarious source and not of God or the universe. The Bible tells us that a character by the name of Accuser, and Liar, disguises himself as a false choice in our lives for the purpose of stealing our freedom from us. This looks like bad habits that you perpetuate in your life, mindsets that keep you stuck, self-deprecation, and a vocabulary filled with malice. Do not allow yourself to settle at a pit stop. There is more to life than what you are currently seeing or experiencing.

If you are happy with where you are that is great, however, if you are desiring more but cannot find it, might I suggest that it's time for you to look in front of you. sometimes the things that are hindering us are the same things that are keeping us from our breakthrough. A breakthrough does not primarily come in the form of stuff or opportunity. We tend to like when that happens however, we are a lot more likely to encounter breakthrough moments in our paradigms before we are to encounter one materialized.

Before you can have your dream life, you have to dream it. Before you can have more money than you know what to do with, you have to have a perspective change about it. Success leaves clues, and certain types of success have different requirements. What it takes to be a rapper is different from what it takes to be a writer. Managing a country as its president is different than managing a business as its CEO which is different than managing a household as a good mother or father. Who you say you are, you become. And the extent at which you become it, is directly correlated to how much you believe that you are it. In life you only receive as much as you believe you are worthy of receiving.

So, who are you? Who do you say you are? What does the fruit of your lips [the words that come from your mouth] say about what you believe think and feel about yourself and the world around you? Are those sentiments genuine? Are you content with your harvest (what you have in your life after taking inventory)? If not, are you willing to change your mind, clear out the roadblock(s), and push forward, as opposed to settling somewhere that was only intended to be a pit stop?

This is where the power of affirmations come in. There is an order of magnitude associated with change. If you can change your mind, then you can change your habits. And if you can change your habits, you can change what you believe, and if you change what you believe, you can change your life for the better. Your life does not change unless your mind changes first. And is not this the conundrum of life? How does changing your mind impact the quality of your life? That question is why I wrote this book. Being receptive to a new way of thinking can open doors that would otherwise remain shut.

Back in March of 2020 I was laid off from my place of employment. At the time I was a contracted recruiter. It was my job to convince people who were at the time already employed, to leave their current job and to start working at the one I was offering to them [at whatever company contracted my place of employment to conduct the talent search]. Prior to that role, so back in 2019, I was in my last year of graduate school for Applied Social and Community Psychology with a counseling and mental health emphasis, and I was caught in the balancing act of school, being an adult and needing a job, and sustaining a rapidly diminishing social life.

From March 2019 to August 2019, I could not keep a job to save my life. The longest stint I had was over night at a clothing warehouse where I would help keep stock; I worked there for about a month. Aside from that role, I went through six other jobs, that's seven in total, and not one was remotely close to being a good fit for me regardless of the task. It was not until mid-August that I landed a job at a liquor store and for a time it was manageable. The environment was welcoming, the pay and the hours were not great, but I could get passed that (especially because at the time I really needed the cash).

In September I accepted the job at the recruiting agency and thought you know what, this could be a step in the right direction. At the time all I wanted was to be able to make ends meet. I was tired of not being able to cover bills every month. I had an apartment and no one in my life at the time had the capacity to lend me money towards my expenses if I needed it. So, I had to hustle and do what I could. That recruiter job at the time was a godsent otherwise I may not have had the gumption to write this book.

I worked that job from September 2019 to March 2020, and what was once a godsent turned into a prayer request that I wanted to be delivered from. Sometimes things are not as they appear, and while I was looking for a big break of sorts, I got instead, mud and trenches. My experience in that role was not all bad however, the tradeoff was becoming insurmountable. Essentially, I was a glorified pencil pusher. 60-100 phone calls a day, some made up script that would have shotty results at best, a boss who would literally not be in the office for weeks at a time, but then would reprimand myself or my colleagues for being literally one minute late to work. Not to mention the office literally had three employees not including my boss and his senior administrator who also happened to be his spouse.

That was the epitome of an unhealthy work environment. The part that would cause the most dissonance in my life was that not only did I struggle in the office, but I also wrestled with challenges at home as well. Yes, my apartment was paid for on time, my fridge remained full, and my social life was improving, but at what cost? I would regularly have to bring my work home where I would dedicate another up to two hours working, not including the commute. And after that, I would still do the quality-of-life things that mattered to me like writing (I was at the beginning stages of starting my blog), playing videogames, cooking (I am a pretty good home chef), and going to the gym.

Eventually I realized that my employment was an albatross around my neck. At the time of that realization, I made a prophetic proclamation that "my current 9-5 would be my last." For me it was not the job itself, but rather it was what the job was costing me: my time, my peace of mind, and my clarity of thought. These things I thought to be invaluable. There was and is nothing that is worth more to me on this side of eternity from a materialistic perspective. You may have heard it before, but money cannot buy time. Your life regardless of your stuff is finite from the perspective of how much time you have to enjoy your existence. As mentioned in an earlier chapter, everyone dies, and when we die our things do not come with us. I had the revelation that my time is worth more than pieces of paper and the stress that comes with them. I had a change of mind. I realized that if I continued to try to climb someone else's latter they would be in charge of how high I could climb, what would be at the top, and whether or not I would be welcomed. I did not want to worship at the altar of a god or gods who were unconcerned about my wellbeing.

That one paradigm shift that came via proxy by the way (sometimes you need outside help to make an inside change), changed the trajectory of my life. When March 2020 rolled around and I was eventually laid off due to the coronavirus pandemic, I was excited to have my time back! Ever since then I have valued it as if it were more precious than gold-because it is. I mentioned my home life at the top of this chapter because for a lot of us self-worth starts at home.

Unfortunately, no one taught me how to value myself properly. No one in the early ages of my life gave me the keys to success. And so, what do you do when you do not know what to do? You settle. You accept that all that you have and all that you know is all that there is to have and know. Sometimes life plateaus. When it does, you have to decide whether or not you are happy with where you have landed. If you are, then your job becomes perpetuating your success-helping others get and gain access to the level of thinking and opportunity that you have. If you are not happy with where life leaves you, get a map and figure out your next destination (have a vision). There are only two directions you can go in life, forward or nowhere; and it's in the plateaus of life, the moments where nothing is happening, that you get to evaluate where you are, and whether or not its satisfying.

The good news, or bad news, depending on how you think about it is, that regardless of where you find yourself you typically cannot go backwards. Rock bottom has a bottom. Wherever you find yourself plateaued at, in most cases, the severity of the situation does not exacerbate unless you allow it to. This is where all those mitigating factors shine: your belief system, your relationships, how you speak to and about yourself, and your capacity to resist. Since leaving my job as a recruiter I have in fact never had another 9-5 proper. And you know what? I do not plan on it either. But that is my resolve. What is important to you? What matters enough to you that you are willing to have an unshakable conviction about it?

This is why what you say matters in relation to manifesting the life that you want. The way you think is only as good as the way you think about what you think. This is called metacognition. Metacognition is when you think about what you are thinking and why you are thinking it.

Sometimes by ourselves, we cannot properly deduce whether or not we are having a beneficial thought. Just because a thought works does not mean that it's right. Consider slavery, just because thinking of a group of people as less than worked from a social and economic perspective for a select few, does not mean that it was the right way of thinking. The other thing to consider, is that the people who were enslaved, also had their own thought process and perspective about their experience. A paradigm or perspective is just a system of thought, and we can sometimes struggle in ourselves because of how that system is formed within us (our personal biases).

This is where cognitive dissonance throws itself into the mix. Cognitive dissonance is when a thought or belief that you have is challenged by another [usually someone else's] thought or belief. These two ideas will do battle internally [inside of you] because they are typically a different side of the same perspective. As an example, imagine you are a gym junky. You go four to five times a week, you have a set regimen that you do, each day has its own body part, and what you are doing is working and you are hitting your goals. Now imagine a friend of yours who also works out regularly but has a different workout schedule than you do. They want to join you on one of your lifts, but your next lift day is legs, and their next day is triceps. Unless there is some concession made by either party, there is and will remain a dissonance from the perspective of workout calendars.

You believe Wednesdays are the best days for leg workouts for you because the planet and stars are aligned just right and at exactly 5:06pm is when you get the best pump. Your friend thinks the exact same thing about Wednesdays but for their triceps. The perspective never changed, you both share the same paradigm of thought that working out is important, the difference is in how you think about that realm of thought.

This is our first roadblock, dealing with our immunity to change. In this scenario you and your friend decide that its best for right now for you two to continue to work out separately. Difference in opinion is a good thing, a lack of receptivity of varying opinions, however, is stifling. The adage that if something is not broken then do not fix it, is a saying unto death. Sometimes the only reason something is not broken is because tape keeps being put on it. Everything needs maintenance including our minds, and that happens when we are unafraid to ask ourselves, "why do I think about this in that way—and what have the results of that mindset been in my life?"

Once you have a grasp on what your convictions are then you can begin to fortify those convictions through affirmations. This is one of the main habits that can be utilized to change your subconscious belief system. The most effective affirmation is an "I am" statement. The idea here is to teach yourself how to speak life over yourself by yourself. When taken seriously, this is a therapeutic type of practice. Here are a few affirmations that I use regularly:

I am so happy grateful and thankful that I am so confident in myself!

I am so happy grateful and thankful that I can accomplish anything that I put my mind to!

I am so happy grateful and thankful that I am successful in all of my endeavors!

Those are just a few, I have more that are more personalized (I would encourage you to do the same). It may seem goofy at first declaring I am this or I am that however, what you are doing is reprograming your mind in the present tense to latch on to a new idea that you formulate about yourself through understanding what matters to you. This is what laying foundation in your life looks like. It's about being willing to get your hands dirty. I used to be uncomfortable in my body. I did not want to be, I just was. I decided one day that "just was" was no longer good enough; so, you know what I did? I spent 30 days in the nude as often as possible.

Changing what you believe can be messy business. That is where those rotten roots are, they are in what and how you believe. That is where habits come in, that is where Living in Alignment comes in, and that is where proactivity is necessary, because that is the valley of the shadow of death. Only you can fix your belief system. Here is where people fall victim to stubbornness, laziness, procrastination, anger issues, insecurities and all the rest. It's because they are unwilling to change what they believe about themselves. Affirmations among other things help with that— but ultimately, this boils down to an identity issue.

The Bible tells us that faith without works is dead. This implies a give and take. For you to gain the fruit of your faith—create the life that you want, you must be willing to work for it. Nothing that happens by surprise comes by surprise. Work goes in on the back end of something for that something to manifest itself on the front end. This is what it means to manifest something into your life. It means that the totality of your being is going towards bringing something to fruition. That's the work required in having a vision. It's as easy as fake it till you make it—will it until you do it.

This is where who you are determines how far you go in life. Your identity matters if for no other reason than you are a unique individual with a one of a kind set of circumstances, that define only your life and no one else's on the planet earth no matter how similar, that you have to navigate because only you are and will ever be you. You must know who you are and what works for you. sometimes you can get so caught up in being everything for everyone else, that you forget how to be enough for yourself. You have the power to determine the trajectory of your life.

Here is the truth: You, are special. You are unique. You are capable, and you are able. You can do anything you put your mind to and you are more powerful than you can even imagine. You have purpose. You are not a waste of space, in fact, the space that you inhabit was created for you. The universe is conspiring on your behalf, and God is looking to give you the desires of your heart-the ones he gave you. Change your mind, change your habits, change your beliefs–change your life for the better.

Chapter 8

The Man Who Chose to Live Out of Alignment

There once was a certain man to which the world was his oyster. He was a natural born musician, an eloquent public speaker, a dynamic problem solver, and an eligible bachelor. This man was full of potential. Money liked him and he liked money. He would hardly ever shy away from a lavish expense. Contrast to all that lavishness, however, was a dark side. Beyond the surface of this man's posterity, boisterousness, and indiscretion, he struggled internally. No, the money was not the problem, the stuff was awesome, and the clout was intoxicating... but there was a lack of fulfillment.

This man was accomplished, but his accomplishments were not satisfactory. The truth is little Stevie never wanted to become a paragon of wealth, success, and achievement, he just wanted to chase opportunity more than he wanted to stay in destitution. But now Stevie is "Steve" (birth name Steven), and Steve has his nose too high up in the air to reduce himself to his roots. He avoids the paparazzi like the plague. After speaking engagements he does not stay beyond the time that was purchased from him; and his fan engagement has been diminishing in quality for some time now.

There is a disconnect between where Steve is now and how he got there. You see, the true measure of success is the value one places on the journey. Once you are in your promise land the only thing that keeps the land looking vibrant years after you inhabit it, is being able to reflect fondly on how you got there. Steve had a distaste for his past. He did not like where he came from—yet he could not get passed that enough to enjoy where he currently was.

So Steve, tormented by his inability to be satisfied with the circumstances of his life, decided that to alleviate the dissonance that he was feeling, he would start a charity for giving to the poor and less fortunate. Steve started the "Steve Gives Back Organization," and through his philanthropic efforts, he excelled at giving out of his abundance all that he had and all of who he was. He met a significant other named Rachel on a trip to Africa where they worked together helping people have access to clean water. The two eventually got married and it seemed as though his philanthropic endeavors were as fruitful if not more so than his other ones.

One day Steve was invited to do a TV interview being conducted by his hometown news station. Initially Steve was reluctant. He had not been in the public eye too much recently, but his philanthropy was starting to get good press. Additionally, the thought of going to his hometown to do an interview was keeping him up at night. He earnestly did not know how to feel. On one hand he wanted to go home, and he wanted the publicity for his philanthropy. On the other hand however, things were going relatively well for him emotionally at this point in his life and he did not want to rock the boat. Ultimately Steve decided to do the interview rationalizing it as not being about him, but rather about platforming the thousands of lives he's had the opportunity to impact in a heartfelt and meaningful way.

During the interview the reporter asked, "you know Stevie, your accomplishments are pretty remarkable. What you are doing beyond the confines of your borders is literally life changing. I must ask you, how have you perpetuated your impact here at home?"

The reporter did not know "Stevie" would be triggering for Steve or that his question in general would cause a bitter response from him.

Steve sat there quietly for a moment, looked up at the reporter and said, "life is available to those who are willing to take it."

The reporter was confused by the response and tried to press Steve on it, but he refused to speak any further on the subject matter.

Later that night, while he was with his wife, Steve watched the interview back and he was mortified by his behavior. He heard his response to the reporter's question and realized that he never changed. He had been all over the world feeding people, clothing people, entertaining people, and pontificating with proficiency; but in a moment where he was triggered, he saw how far he had not come.

What we do not see in that interview moment is that when Steve heard "Stevie," that was the first time he allowed anyone to call him that outside of a specific group of people in years. The interviewer did not know him well enough to be that informal with him, and to Steve, someone from his hometown outside of his immediate family calling him "Stevie" must want to roll their sleeves up and step outside. An innocent moment instantly became a battlefield. Steve's response came out of a place of survival. The million-dollar question here is why did Steve in that moment of being called the nickname he's had for decades, feel as though he needed to protect himself?

Steve never shared this with anyone, not even Rachel, but growing up, Stevie was a chump. He was bullied, thrown into lockers, and overlooked by his friends, family, and relatives. No one gave Stevie a second thought let alone a first one; and this was the case for most of his early life.

Stevie wanted to become Steve for a long time, but his moment never came. Stevie felt as though he could never mess up, and that he always had to perform so that people would feed him the real thing that he craved the most-attention. Steve was a champion because he liked the attention, he was a perfectionist because of the notoriety, and he liked doing for others because it's what made him feel good. Steve had no sense of sacrifice. No aptitude for servitude.

So yes, while his career and life catapulted from one level of success to another through his charitable work; he kept missing the mark of his spiritual purpose. Steve kept being [proverbially] hungry because he kept eating "food" that was not filling. The real kicker here, is that Steve's greatest pain point was also his biggest breakthrough opportunity. Steve used to dream about going home and helping his family, friends, and locals in the community. He would envision starting a community center and setting up a business headquarters there.

He allowed the disappointments of his life to drown out a desire for his destiny. This was a jarring revelation for Steve, and he fell into the abyss. He was chronically depressed for months, wrestled with resentment and forgiveness, and had a general sense of a lack of direction. He and Rachel fell out of love with each other. They separated and ultimately divorced; she took their three kids.

Steve took a step back from his philanthropic work and hired someone to manage those affairs for him. His reputation also took a dramatic hit after his downward spiral and a whirlwind of bad press. Steve became Stevie again. One day he sat back and wondered to himself why he was so eager to leave where he came from in the first place. He determined that the motivating factor for him was that he did not want to become like the people who stayed. But in the end, Steve did stay. Steve left home, but home never left him.

My main takeaway from this story for you is to find purpose in your pain. In life all of us are susceptible to getting hurt, however, pain does not have to be debilitating. You can recover and overcome. Living in Alignment is not pain management, its rehabilitation. Your alignment journey is a choice to improve and not stay the same. You must learn to grow through your pain. This means you must learn to give your pain meaning. Do not say hurt-heal and get better.

Chapter 9

Mental Health Matters

Your mind is the literal center of your universe. Signals channel up and down your neural pathways to and from your brain dictating to you how you should interact with the world around you, forming your sense of reality. The primary function of your mind is to allow you to experience life in essence. What do I mean? Our brain's focus in addition to helping us accomplish everyday tasks, is on determining sensations and environmental stimuli. The various lobes of our brain work to help us interpret what is happening to us in any given moment. Your brain tells you when something is pleasurable, euphoric, painful or unsafe. Having a base level understanding of how your brain operates in this way is key in decerning your decision-making process.

One of the most cataclysmic choices that a human ever made is in the Bible's account of human creation. In the book of Genesis it says that after God made Adam and Eve, he specifically told them not to eat of the tree of the knowledge of good and evil less they die (the implication being a slow death, for example, living to be 75 or 80 years old). Ultimately, they decided to eat from the tree of the knowledge of good and evil because the fruit appeared suitable for their consumption.

Your choices have such a heavy impact on your future because your choices are a response to your senses. Our minds serve us to the primary purpose of being and staying alive. From a nature perspective, humans are survivalists. On a fundamental level all we know how to do is prolong life. The signals that your brain sends you in response to what you are exposed to externally will dictate how you react in a moment. And how you react in that moment can have far reaching repercussions. Have you ever done something that in the moment did not seem like that big of a deal, but later ended up coming back and being a huge deal? When that happens, it's called a consequence. Every decision has a consequence and every consequence that comes to pass influences the direction of your future. Think of it like a river that has multiple offshoots into various streams. Each stream represents a different choice made and the ramifications thereof-the path that the water (your life) objectively takes.

In the same way, how far we go in life is directly predicated on the choices we make based on the response our brain tells us to have when in contact with/in the presence of various environmental stimuli. Making a decision is always more than half the battle. In a lot of cases, the right time is when you say it is. Sometimes growth is objective meaning we have to go through something, we have to experience something, or we have to live through some type of life event to get to the revelation on the other side. Other times however, growth is subjective-you have to decide to do so. After Adam and Eve betrayed God and ate of the fruit of the knowledge of good and evil, and realized what they had done; the Bible says that they hid from God when he came in search of them. When God finds them we find out that it was a conscious choice of Adam and Eve to hide from God instead of being open and honest with their mistake. A bad decision has the potential to obliterate your quality of life. This is why mental health matters on a functional level—if you do not know how to make a wise decision you will not make one, and if you do not make a wise decision where one would count, you could end up in an exigent situation.

How to Have a Better Decision-Making Process

One of the ways to avoid the calamity of a bad decision is to be able to parse through what your brain is telling you. This can be accomplished via mindfulness. I know sometimes mindfulness can get a bad rep for being misused and overvalued however, this is in part because subscribers to mindfulness are more so parishioners of a "faith," as opposed to users of a tool. Within the framework of psychology, mindfulness or being mindful, is a type of introspection that forces you to reflect on yourself within the context of what you are experiencing in real time, as opposed to projecting–emoting for the sake of survival. Mindfulness is about looking at a subjective response objectively: "why in response to that did I do this or feel that?" You live with you more than anyone else does, the least you can do is understand what makes you tick. Why do you personally take offense when you hear a socially derogatory term? What would make you cross the street indiscriminately at the sight of a group of black men? What made you think that someone who was not talking about you actually was? Mindfulness is having a clear and rational consensus of self. Knowing who you are is deeper than knowing what you want, it's about knowing why you want it.

As this relates to choice and making better decisions, mindfulness can help on multiple fronts. Over the course of time being intrinsically self-aware lends itself to the decision-making process in that for starters, you will know how to say "no." At some point in your journey "no" should become your best friend. Successful people will tell you that saying "no" more frequently than "yes" is a critical part of success. "No" will keep you out of things that you have no business being a part of in the first place. It's important that "no" is your friend and that you keep its number on speed dial. It's not enough to know "no," you have to be able to say it: "no, I am unavailable on that day," "no, that does not sound like a good idea to me," "no I cannot, maybe next time," "No." This is about being lord over your time. The only true currency that we have is our attention, and our attention costs us time. The phrase "pay attention" literally means to give whatever that is in front of you your focus. Your focus always comes with a plus one, your time. You may be losing your mind because you are giving your attention to the wrong things. "Seeing the bright side" is a literal life or death prognosis, that is, being able to do so versus an inability wherein.

Hope is the Spice of Life

Having a certain degree of self-awareness also aids in the development of your belief process. Change your mind, change your behavior, change your beliefs—then you will have changed your life for the better. You only receive what you believe you are worthy of receiving. Self-awareness through mindfulness is all about getting down to your "Why." I talked about this in a previous chapter, but essentially your "why," is the reason you get out of bed in the morning. It's the reason when you tried giving up on your dream, your dream did not give up on you. It's your stamina. It not only gets you up and going, but it also keeps you up and going.

Its hope!

Your life is only as good (qualitatively) as your hope. Your hope directs your life, but your mind directs your hope. This is what I meant by "seeing the bright side" as being a life-or-death prognosis, because if you can see a bright side, your situation will have a bright side. But if you cannot see beyond a triggered emotional and or physiological response, your quality of life will diminish due to a lack of light in those dark areas.

A key takeaway here is that thriving, and surviving are two different things that are also codependent of one another. To thrive means to flourish, to prosper, be fortunate and or successful. To survive means to remain. The only way to remain anywhere, is to be somewhere that is flourishing. Something in your life has to be going well at any given time. God or the universe will not just pull the rug from under your feet. If your finances are not where you would like them to be, at least you are healthy. If your health is not the best at least you are alive. "It could always be worse" is a spiritual principle to live by. You are not doing as bad as you think you are. There is a bright side, you just may not be looking at it. You are not crazy necessarily, maybe it's just the people around you. Sometimes it's healthy to change your surroundings.

You may be asking yourself, "but what does all of this have to do with my material health?" Simply put, successful people affect life while unsuccessful people allow life to affect them. The only way you can affect life is through your mind. How you respond to what you experience will impact what happens next in your life, AKA consequences. The consequences of your life directly impact your material health by influencing your quality of life (what your life is objectively, how you think about that reality, and your sense of hope within that context).

Chapter 10

Relationships

Now, let's talk relationships. Whether romantic, plutonic, or otherwise, relationships are an integral part of the human condition. All of us whether we want to or not must interact with people. It's a prerequisite to existence. You cannot do anything without encountering another human being at one point or another. I am going to breakdown for you the moving pieces involved in any relationship, so that you can gain a better understanding of what is taking place in your relationships, what areas of improvement you could be working on, and how to maintain and sustain healthy relationships. Knowledge of this will help you in your success journey because it will enable you to better navigate the inevitable pitfalls of human interaction.

The most obvious place to start when discussing the dynamics of your relationships is your family. Your family is the first real relationship that you are ever in. You are born into this relationship. Your mother thinks a certain way about you, your father has his own perception of you, your brother(s), sister(s), cousin(s), aunt(s), and uncle(s) all have their own thoughts when it comes to you, and you them. It's within the family where you are supposed to gain an understanding of the concept of love (more on that later), and how to function and operate in it. A healthy family environment bares the fruit of a healthy personal relationship life. A dysfunctional family environment will produce dysfunctional and sporadic personal relationships. If you do not know better you will not know how to do better, and it's within your family where you learn how to care, where you learn how to cherish, where you learn your core values around respect for persons, and where you learn to respect yourself.

You are a conduit for your experiences, even in your relationships. You relive in real time what you were exposed to in the past. What makes you closed off to someone new is the hurt that someone similar caused you. What attracts you to a specific type of person is in some cases the same thing that turns you off about someone else. Or maybe you like a person because they demonstrate qualities that someone previous in your life did not have. These relational loops and cycles play out in our lives in constant rotation but in various and different forms; daddy issues can almost be diagnosable. But it does not stop there because the next thing that you get from your family in addition to a crash course in love and care, is a comprehension of support.

Most people know what it means to be supported. You may have felt or been supported before, shown your support for someone else, or maybe even, have felt a lack of support and know what it's like to want or need someone in your corner. Think of the word support in a literal sense. We all need someone who is foundational in our lives and or serves the purpose of being able to help us stand in our times of need and vulnerability. A family has its own built in support structure. Sometimes it's a singular person, where the only time you see your relatives is when your mom or aunt calls you all together. Sometimes the support is a mindset where the entire family shares in the same core values and beliefs. It could be geographical where the only thing that keeps your family together is the fact that you all live within the same vicinity of one another.

Beyond this base level of compliance amongst a group of individuals the next tier of support comes from things (behaviors) that are actionable. You can tell when you are being supported. Often when a person cares, they will demonstrate that care. Consideration is a verb and support is the way in which it functions-having someone who will sit down and listen to you. Being with people who are willing and able to catch you when you fall. Or honestly just having someone show up when you need them in a tangible way. This is actionable support. The best way to think of this is, there are probably some people in your life that you have no problem in asking for money from.

There will not be a big deal around it, you and they have an agreement, and you know that the transaction is on a mutual footing and understanding of one another. On the other hand, there are probably also some people in your life that you would not think twice about asking for money from. This is not because you love or care for them any less, but rather you just know that they do not support you in that way. They will probably blow everything out of proportion and make $20 feel like you asked for $2000. Or maybe they have loose lips and asking them means asking your entire social network. Support stands on its own, and anything that cannot is intrinsically unsupportive.

THE PURSUIT OF PASSION

Once again, because we learn what support is based on what we are exposed to in our family, that has a direct effect on our external relationships-those outside of our familial structure. A bad relationship will always feel better than a worse one, and a good relationship will make you not want to get back into a bad one (in most cases). This is where your friends, associates, comrades, and the like come into play. The Bible tells us that two people do not walk together unless they have agreed to; your social relationships are supports that you build around and for yourself. This is why you can be friends with two people, but those same two people do not get along with one another; they have no reason to walk together, beyond you. And the only reason why you are walking with them is because they are of direct help (support) in some way to you.

In nature these types of relationships are called symbiotic relationships. There are three types of symbiotic relationships: mutual, common, and parasitic. Mutualism is when two different species are both benefiting from their relationship.

Commensalism is when only one species benefits from a relationship, and parasitism is when one species benefits from the relationship, but at the cost of the other party involved. In a perfect world we should all be striving for mutually beneficial relationships; however, it's more likely that more of your relationships will fall in the commensalism or even parasitism realm of symbiosis. This is because human beings are self-serving survivalists, so a lot of times a perfect world is not always conducive with another man or woman's direct survival. You do not negotiate with your food before you eat it. In the same way not every relationship will be mutually beneficial.

In fact, most of our relationships are transaction driven making it difficult to truly value the people we come across in our daily lives as individuals. This desensitization of being able to see individuality in others is also exacerbated by how we see people treated around us. We are constantly inundated by media with all kinds of hate pornography that fetichize intolerance and in

THE PURSUIT OF PASSION

some cases promotes a personality trait of being against someone just for the sake of it.

Should doing as the Romans do still apply if you are in a racist environment? What if you are in a workplace that has a certain stigma that you do not share? Or what if you are the one people are constantly looking down on you with contempt?

In these types of [common and parasitic] relationships and environments, you are only as good as what you contribute. This is what I call "Transactionalism," the art of going along to get along. I used to have a boss that would say, "it's not what you have done, it's what have you done for me recently?" Mutualism is a shared general concern that serves as a unifier for the benefit of two or more people; "transactionalism" through commensalism and parasitism, is a general concern for self-facilitated through one's engagement with others. Sometimes a person's desire is not to get along with you, but rather to use you.

Next let's focus on romantic relationships. Romantic relationships are interesting because they are biological in nature. Humans are biologically wired through the chemicals in our brains to fall in love. A significant other serves the purpose in your life of providing you with a sense of bliss, euphoria, and connection. That special someone in your life is supposed to be the person that you morph your life together with, to create something that is greater than the sum of its parts. Some people get really attached in romantic relationships being so into the other person that they lose themselves. Some know how to strike that healthy balance of care, support, and consideration that makes every day feel brand new. And some romantic relationships are thrill rides constantly throwing the people involved to and fro. This is not a dating column or an intro lesson on marriage, but what I am trying to impress on you is that at this level, who you have in your life matters.

Beyond the vanity of sexual attraction who you have as your spouse can make all the difference in the trajectory of your life. In the Bible there is a story about this man named Job. He was a wise and faithful man who loved the Lord. One day he became a target for Satan and was left desolate and without any of his worldly possessions. Even still, he (Job) remained committed to God to the point where his wife got so irritated with him that she told him to curse God and die. Thank God Job did not listen to her because if he had, his story would have turned out differently. The person who is in your corner should be in your corner.

Do not be unevenly yoked meaning, do not subjugate yourself to 70/30, 60/40, or 80/20 relationships where you are always the one carrying the heavier load. In any serious romantic relationship, both parties should be all in–100%. That means both of you are giving 100% of your time. Both of you are equally putting in 100% of your effort. And both of you are using 100% of your strength and energy to carry the load of the relationship together. Your romantic relationship should be one that is truly of mutual benefit. This is a testament of wholeness. You do not want to be in any position where someone is one foot in one foot out as it comes to you. Oh, but you love that person? It's okay to love from a distance. This is one of the areas of traversing the road to success that people will trip up on.

Sometimes the person(s) you are holding on to is the same one(s) keeping you stuck and stagnant. Not everyone in your life is or will be encouraged and inspired that you are doing the work necessary to better yourself—spouse included. Sometimes the best thing you can do for yourself, and that person, is to create space physically, emotionally, or otherwise. You can still love and care for that person, but sometimes during your growth journey you may come to a place where being too close in vicinity with a specific person or group of people only leads to toxic or abusive behavior that is not good for you, or the other person(s) involved.

Just because you are growing does not mean you have to let go of those you love and care for. Space is not as scary as it may sound, and creating space is better than remaining in an unhealthy or potentially dangerous situation. Additionally, on the flip side, anyone who truly loves and cares for you will not try to hold you back from being all that you desire to be. The truth of the matter is people come in your life for a reason, a season, or a lifetime; and too many times especially in our romantic lives, people will have a tendency to give someone lifetime access that was only supposed to have a season pass. Anyone who does not stay in your life was never meant for your life in the first place. You must learn to be okay with letting people go. Whether it be you leaving them or them leaving you, if that person is no longer in your life regardless of the type of relationship, be okay with the fact that their time, and that time, is up.

You have to be able to compartmentalize what a person means to you. What do I mean? This may sound messed up, but ask yourself objectively, "how important is that relationship really?" Sometimes people will hold on to a relationship just because they have history via shared experiences. The issue that tends to pop up with this type of trauma link is, as one person grows the other person cannot or refuses to acknowledge that person's growth, because they themselves might not be growing in a way they would like to. Because of that, they are envious and feel resentment and insecurity. Sometimes the best thing you can do while manifesting your desires is keep your mouth shut.

Not everyone can handle the fullness of who you are. Those people will turn on you, not take advice from you, and possibly even plot against you. In laymen terms those people are haters. They were never really for you. They liked you when you were down because you were down with them. Now that you are working to get your life together suddenly there is a problem... There is no problem, they just do not want to see you do better than them. The people that do not want you to shine brighter than them will work overtime to try to dem your light. Regardless of good will, helping those type of people in your life is futile. Just because a person tolerates having you around does not mean they want you around.

Treating the people in your life with a degree of objectivity keeps them from lording over you. People who cannot go where you can, will try to keep you from going. Remember that you are responsible for your own quality of life—you only receive what you believe you are worthy of receiving. If you do not believe you can find someone better, you will not. If you believe that your ambition can only go as high as someone else's ceiling for your life, then that will be your reality. No one meaningful in your life should actively try or want to keep you from being all that you were created to be. Sometimes you have to stand in the gap for yourself, advocate for yourself, and find a degree of fidelity with yourself that will hold you and those you have or invite into your life to a higher standard.

Another concept that people can have an issue within this area of their life is a misnomer of excellence. There is nothing wrong with setting a standard. Contentment is the key to a happy life however, "content" and "tolerate" are not synonyms. It's more than okay to want more from your relationships especially if you are doing the inner work that you need to be doing for yourself. The Bible tells us that a friend sharpens a friend, like iron sharpening itself. It's okay to not want to have dull people in your circle. Dull does not mean boring or uninteresting, it means people who do not have anything going for them. They may be kind, nice, and caring folk however, if the context of their conversation does not go past the block they live on, then it's okay to have to need to expand your horizons. This does not mean you love or care for them any less, especially if it's a spouse or significant other, but it does mean that you are going to have to develop and grow in the people who you associate with.

Success in your relationships familial, plutonic, romantic, or otherwise, is predicated on the importance that you place on them. This goes both ways. Less important relationships do not need to be kept alive if they are ultimately taking you nowhere. And your important relationships need constant maintenance if you intend to keep them important. I think that is one of the biggest takeaways from this chapter, a successful relationship is a mutually beneficial relationship wherein the parties involved are committed to the growth process. This helps you in your success journey because, it's better to have someone who is for you, regardless of who is against you, as opposed to facing a bunch of opposition completely alone. You will know that you are in sync with your success by the opposition that will come your way; and as it comes, you are going to want to know that someone is in your corner.

Finally, I want to address love. Love is the unspoken language. It makes you smile just thinking about it. It's warmth, solidarity, communion, and understanding. The Bible tells us that love is patient and kind, not envious, boastful, or proud. It's important to understand love because it's the universal support. What makes a mother want to take care of her daughter? What makes a dad want to play catch with his son? What makes two people decide to walk down the aisle together? Love. You can feel love with a complete stranger and feel no love from people you have known for years. Love is among other things a willingness to know and be known.

We all have a frame of reference for love. Typically, this comes from how we encounter love in our families. Also and however, as mentioned earlier, there is a biological component to love as well that dictates to us what love should "feel" like. It's this base level understanding of love that we take with us every day to school, the workplace, the party, and various other social engagements. You use this foundational framework of love to build your life. It's important to know how you operate within the context of love. Love is not bias, nor does it discriminate. You do not have to be in a committed relationship to know love. Each of us have our own love language-how we express and receive love best. One way to think of this is as "base stats."

In a role-playing game you get to play as a character that has base stats. Base stats refer to what that character is good at without any training or equipment. As an example, a typical role-playing game may have a standard of four base stats: health, attack, defense, and speed. Of the playable characters, one character may have naturally good attack, decent defense, but not a lot of health or speed. Another character may have a lot of attack and speed, but bad health and defense. A third character may have good health and defense but is very slow and does not deal a lot of damage, so on and so forth. In a similar way, there are several different ways to express love and you have a certain level of aptitude in each "skill/ability" available. The five love languages (base stats of love) are: words of affirmation, acts of service, receiving/giving gifts, quality time, and physical touch.

When you learn and understand how you flow in love, and how love flow towards you (think vibrational frequency), that is when you will begin to see success in this area of your life, and subsequently, the rest. Success is the persistent daily practice of simple principles and disciplines. You should be growing in your love daily. Love for yourself and love for others. How you grow in this area is by not deciding to love less (which can happen after being hurt several times) but rather, by being intentional with how you love on those who you come in contact with.

Not everyone needs all your time, can you demonstrate your love for someone in five minutes? If you are a giver, are you giving with the recipient in mind? Will they actually like what you got them? If you like physical contact, can you engage in healthy touching and not something potentially offensive? When you grow in your love language you grow in your effectiveness. And when you grow in your effectiveness you grow in your usefulness. And the more useful you are, the more opportunities and breakthroughs will come your way.

Chapter 11

The Business of Life

It does not matter what you do it matters who you are. Say you are invited to a dinner party, and you meet some new people for the first time. One of the first questions that is likely to be asked is, "what do you do for a living?" I loathe this question. People have become so accustomed with associating their identity with how they contribute to society.

You are not your job. In fact, you make your job what it is. Sure, they could hire someone else, but who they would bring on would not be able to do what you do like you do or how. Your uniqueness goes beyond who you push pencils for or who signs your paycheck. You are a spiritual being having a physical experience meaning there is more to you than meets the eye. Your thoughts matter, your words matter, and your opinions matter. Life will not always put a proper evaluation on you. That is why it's important that you value yourself. One of the ways you do this is by valuing your time.

Stop doing things that you do not want to do. The reason why you hate getting up for work in the morning is because you hate your job. Do something you love, and you will never work another day in your life. Are you doing something you love with your life? An overwhelming number of people report being disengaged at their place of employment; meaning while they are at work, they would rather be somewhere else. Is that you? Or maybe you do love what you do. That is fantastic. How are you perpetuating an amicable environment for your fellow employees? Are you contributing to a healthy workplace or are you keeping your head down and going home at the end of your shift without making a tangible difference to and with those around you?

The Bible says that your gifts will make room for you. Are your skills, talents, and abilities giving way to bigger and better opportunities in your life? This is why who you are is more important than what you do because you have to bring you with you everywhere you go. You cannot walk out of your front door and leave you at home. Jobs come and go, there will always be work to do, but the real work is the inner work. Self-development will sustain you where skills and talents cannot. You could be one of the best accountants in the office, but if you have a crummy attitude, you will miss opportunities that are meant to come your way.

It's not what you know it's who you know. This is truer today than ever before. Your altitude is connected to your contact list. Who is in your network that can open doors for you, and who is in your network that is willing to do so? Who you befriend matters, and how you present yourself matters. Your associations are the last real thing that make you stand out. You cannot hang out with everyone because not everyone is good for you to hang out with. Finding your place in the world starts by finding your place within yourself.

I think it's fascinating how people will intentionally go out of their way to spend less time with themselves. Surely you have encountered this person before, or maybe you are this type of person: they can never be by themselves, are always on the go, and are always up to something new. This is called instability. When someone cannot be with themselves it's usually because there is something there that they are trying to avoid. Peace in part comes from inner knowing. You will know you are at peace when things are peaceful. Self-avoidance is not sustainable and is often built like a house of cards—just one wrong move, and it can all come tumbling down.

Life will not always be in your favor, your job will not always have you in line for the next promotion, and your friends and peers behind closed doors, can be just as crazy as you. You must help yourself advance. Growth is not à la carte. You are going to have to get in the kitchen and cook this meal for yourself. When you are not reading this book, how are you continuing education? How are you developing your skillsets? After you clock out of work, what are you doing for yourself? This is where growth takes place, in the margins of our lives.

The older you get, the more intentional you have to be about what you want. Doors tend to open less frequently as you get settled into adult life. As kids, middle schoolers, high schoolers, and sometimes even through under grad, it can feel as though the world was created for you. The stars are always in alignment for you, and every door you knock on opens and greets you with open arms. As we become adults however, the perks of our youthfulness begins to expire because suddenly society has a higher expectation of us. As an able-bodied adult it's up to you to create your reality. As a kid you lived in someone else's world and was exposed to what they wanted to expose you to. As an adult, you have to expose yourself to what you want to be exposed to.

This is where perseverance and resilience come into play, because creating a path for yourself is not easy. We are told that anyone can step out on their own which is true in America however, just because you step out on your own two feet does not mean you are strong enough to sustain where you stand; and without support? Forget about it. This is why it's important to have goals, hopes, and a vision. A vision will outlive a situation. And hope gives you a real reason to get out of bed beyond a piece of intrinsically worthless paper. Essentially, you have to want more for yourself. The Bible says that you have not because you ask not. Stop not asking for things. Your life stagnates when you stagnate. You decide whether or not to push forward, or to die where you stand. The only way you fail is if you quit, so stop quitting.

Sometimes you may wonder when is it my turn, when is my breakthrough coming, or when will there be a turnaround in my life? I will tell you when, when you go back and pick up that thing that you may have put down years ago. We all have a "proper" or pre-destined path for our lives (that is where our desires come from). The question is never will you become what you are supposed to, it's always to what degree? The difference here is the size of a chasm. How short will you fall or how close will you get to realizing your potential? Detours and reroutes are part of life. Sometimes unfortunate things happen that you may not have been expecting and you just have to roll with the punches. That's one thing; but it's something else to self-sabotage and be the source of your own delay. Quitters never win because they are never in the competition long enough. The one thing that the laws of nature will respect above all else is longevity. Do you have the power to stick with what you start? If you hang out long enough somebody will notice you. Even the last person gets picked eventually.

Something that someone once said that stuck with me was, "if you ever need a job, just show up to the place you want to work and start doing the job you want to be hired for. Eventually someone will inquire about your employment and maybe even want to hire you." Now I doubt this is an effective strategy for getting a job in the 21st century however, the sentiment of this idea remains: make yourself stand out until you are invited in. And if you are never invited in the conventional way, at least you will have paved your own way, which in some cases is better anyway.

Chapter 12

Heavy is the Head

The same people who cheer you will be the same ones that will jeer you. When you make it to the mountain top, do not get comfortable, because eventually you will be in the valley again. Never get too close to the sun otherwise you may burn. Stay grounded. Keep the principles that got you here. These are all key lessons that come with living with fidelity. The success journey is about becoming all that you were created to be. Not mediocre, and certainly not average. Does that mean you have a mansion and four car garage? No not necessarily. What it means is, whatever you discover as your purpose, you are determined to experience it in its fullness. There are active forces that want to keep you from doing exactly that. Success does not have barriers in and of itself, but there are barriers to success.

Sustaining where life takes you is about knowing how to whether the storm. There is a time to be active, and a time to be still. A time to move to the next check point, and a time to linger for a while. Do not be in a rush to grow up too fast, but at the same time, do not wait until near death before you start having a life. Responsibilities are a good thing. Think of them as your reward, a badge of honor, for making it to a new level. Seek them out humbly, do not take them on haphazardly. It's okay to say "no." It's okay to be a history revisionist—not everyone needs the whole story. Implement the 80/20 rule. Not everyone needs all your time, but for the few who do, do not leave anything on the table. Legacies come in all shapes and sizes, but that is your true crown. Who did you

THE PURSUIT OF PASSION

help while you were here? Who is better because they got to know you? No "why" means no direction. Directionless people are stagnant people because they have nowhere to go.

Figure out what makes you tick. Go on a retreat/sabbatical. Get away from yourself for a few and see what you find when you are not busy being you. No one ever always has that much going on; take a break—even God rested. Stand for something less you fall for everything. Believe in your future more than your past. Your better days are always the one's you have left, not the ones that have gone by. Know when enough is enough. Limits and boundaries are a good thing. Too many however, can paralyze you. Walk with wisdom. Sometimes it's better to ask for forgiveness than permission.

Trust your gut, it's your intuition. Even if your gut feeling is wrong, there is more social cachet in standing firm in what you believe than in appearing spineless. Yes, some things are that serious. Yes, deep people do in fact drown. Learn to strike a balance between theory and practice (what could be versus what is). Living in the moment means disconnecting from the internet and being present for real life. You should not be a jack of all trades, but rather a master of one, learning. You are a life learner. Schooling does not stop after high school or college; it just comes in different forms. The reason you do not take into consideration that what you may be going through is merely a test in the school of life, is because people tend to disassociate a formal education with knowing how to be adaptable. The Bible says that contentment is the secret of life; In all my schooling (and there is a lot), I have never taken a contentment 101 course, but I have learned some things from life itself.

Individuation is a survival tactic. In some instances, the correct thing to do is to go down with the ship. But never be afraid to abandon ship if you do not trust the captain. The only way you lose is if you quit. You will always see a reason to stop prematurely before you see a reason to keep moving forward. If you do not know what to do, it's okay to do nothing until you do. Do not intentionally offend. But also, do not wavier in your convictions. Your convictions are an internal GPS, follow them.

You will probably spend a good portion of your time in the waiting room of life, so know how to wait well. Not everything requires an immediate response. Let people think what they want about you, it's none of your business anyway; anyone with an ounce of dignity will approach you directly if necessary. It's okay if you get over in some situations, but do not look to try to get over in every area of your life; cheaters never prosper. Nice people may finish last but at least they finish. Slow and steady can in fact win a race.

Conclusion

Make Peace with Your Past

Finally, and in conclusion, above all else, make peace with your past. Forgive what needs to be forgiven. Let go of what needs to be let go of and move on. Sometimes you can be your own worst obstacle because you may be holding yourself hostage to something that took place 10 or 15 years ago. You need to realize that thing that you are having a hard time forgiving yourself or someone else for, has already forgiven itself.

Whatever hurt or pain that you went through 12 years ago resolved itself 12 years ago. It happened already. You not being able to make sense of it does not detract from the fact that it's all said and done. Now extend to yourself the grace you need to say, "I may have gone through that, but that does not define me." You are special, valuable, more powerful than you can even imagine, and can accomplish anything you put your mind to.

    I am a personal witness of how living in the past will keep someone from their compelling future. I had a friend who was once wronged by someone, and years after the fact he was never able to move on in his life. After a few drinks and merriment, he would tune his proverbial guitar and start singing the same old sad song of how a certain person hurt him and how his life had never been right since. Do not be like my friend, do not let the hurt you endure live on longer than it has to. I am not saying that hurt did not leave a wound, I am saying stop picking at the scab and let it heal.

    One of the mysteries of life is, you do not know how what you go through will impact your life. And honestly, it's not for us to know. But look at what we do after the fact: mull over time and time again what we went through as if we are experiencing it fresh for the first time after telling the story for the 100th time. We self-traumatize ourselves by reliving what hurt us. You are more than the sum of your experiences. Before you go through anything, you are everything. The Bible says that you are fearfully and wonderfully made, that means, life does not happen to you, you happen to life.

I realize that sometimes life is not fair, bad things happen to good people, and bad people seem to get away with everything, but may I submit to you, that it's not your obligation or responsibility to figure out why something did or did not happen to/for you. You have to have faith for your future. What I mean is, you must believe that your better days are the ones that you have left, and not the ones that have gone by. You must believe that you are a powerful being that can affect life and not just be affected by it. This is how you move forward in life and make peace with your past, by putting it in its proper place-behind you.

Some of what you went through just requires an objective perspective to properly reason with it. Because all humans are self-centered to a more or less degree, a lot of times people tend to experience what they go through as an indictment on their character. Have you ever said to yourself after experiencing something, "why did this happen to me?" People have a tendency to like to take ownership of things that involve, include, or happen around them. Let me help set you free: not everything is about you. Every now and again it's okay to just be a witness. You can be involved with something and not be a part of it at the same time. This is called minding your business. Knowing how and when to mind your business will save your life both literally and metaphorically. Just because others are doing something does not mean that their something automatically has something to do with you. Let go of that insecurity. You are not everyone's hot topic.

An interesting quality about a plurality of animal species is that they have a very short-term memory. One of the ways this plays to their advantage is if for example one animal is attacked by another in the wild. If the animal that is attacked manages to get away, their short-term memory will serve as a coping mechanism. Imagine being a gazelle and getting attacked by a pride of lions while grazing and getting a drink of water from your favorite side of the river bend. You manage to escape the lions attacking you but now you need to go back to the river to finish eating and drinking. As a human you would probably say to yourself "no way, I was just attacked, I cannot go back to that river anymore, I have to go and tell everyone I know what just happened to me and how traumatic it was—I mean a LION just tried to eat me!"

The thing about a gazelle, however, is, they will go back to doing whatever it is they were doing before they were attacked, as if it never happened. There are somethings in your life that happen to you, that you need to be able to just overlook. I am not saying the moment in and of itself was not important but rather, maybe that moment was not that important as it pertains to you. Going back to the gazelle analogy, the gazelle managed to get away, but on the flip side, the lions are returning to their pride empty handed, exhausted, and hungry. You do not know what something means to someone else. This is why being less subjective about what you experience will help you make peace with your past, because it will keep you from making a mountain out of a mole hill.

Making peace with your past is about coming to a decision about its conclusion. You have to decide when you have served a long enough sentence. Whatever hurt you are harboring may be painful and the wound may be deep however, which is more valuable to you: being a conqueror or being conquered? I am not talking to people who have a victim mentality. I am talking to people who if they get knocked down seven times, they will get up eight. It takes courage and tenacity to say, "my life did not stop after that person wronged me years ago." It takes boldness to stand in the face of your mistakes and say, "you do not own me anymore." Misery loves company and hoping can hurt however, do you want to die where you stand or move forward towards a better future? That is the true choice on the table every time you rehearse your past.

Acknowledgments

Giving honor to Jesus Christ my Lord and Savior. The Bible says that we are overcomers by the blood of Jesus and by the word of our testimony. Sharing my experiences is a big part of my walk in becoming more like Christ. To be clear, this is not a Christian book even though I reference the Bible in it. I did That with intentionality because the Bible is spiritual literature and one of the key points of this book is to engage with your spiritual self. As a disclaimer I am not intentionally trying to evangelize you or propagandize Christianity however, I must properly acknowledge the one who has enabled me to do exceedingly abundantly more than I was able to conceive or imagine on my own.

I also want to acknowledge the women who have supported me along the way: Valarie, Brenda, Shirley, Rose, Elizabeth, Penny, Angela, Syreeta, Khi, Brittany, and Sherri.

As a final thought I would encourage you to stay humble. The Bible says that the greatest among you is the least. Pride comes before the fall, and a sure-fire way to fall is to think too highly of yourself. At the end of the day, there is no difference between you, and the homeless person you pass on your way to your job, home, or social engagement. We are all subject to Maslow's Hierarchy of Needs, and anything beyond that is vanity. As you climb the proverbial latter of your success, do not forget to reach back to help someone get to where you are.

About the Author

Tiffany Jerome is the author's pseudonym. The author chose to use a pseudonym for this book because of its symbolic spiritual significance. In spiritual texts you often read about people being given spiritual names. In chapter 3 of this book, the author references the existence of a spiritual you. When you are willing to engage with yourself in an inquisitive way sometimes what comes forth can be revelatory. Tiffany Jerome means "The Manifestation of God a Sacred Name."

www.ingramcontent.com/pod-product-compliance
Lightning Source LLC
Chambersburg PA
CBHW072053110526
44590CB00018B/3145